[Document consists of overlapping handwritten manuscript pages in French, 18th century cursive. Partial transcription of legible portions:]

Top document

...residant en...
...jalgnin, listentié bois, aulieu de...
de la ville de Cormeil, y demeurant, le q...
redstétairement relourié, et laissé, avoir vendu
cédé, quitté et transporté, et maintenant appar-
toujours quittes et... de mes diviers noël avocat
à labour... en la Bailliage, demeurant
En cette ville et de Damme marguerite de fay
son Espouse, du dit... son mary bien et dument
licentiée, et authorisée à leffet des presente, le-
quelle à dispre retenuelle pour agreable, ce
present, stipulant, et acceptant pour... leurs
hoirs, ...sesseurs, ou ayant cause, lefond et
tréfonds des heritages cy apres detaillés, scavoir
situés au Bourg de fagny...
... de diedrer, scavoir la moitié...
situer au dit lieu, en la ...suivants
...ieux à droite En venant de...
...chappois y constais lavez...
...levaudoulé...

Right edge

...ardenne
...residant à...
...ente present, En leurs per-
...ent soumis René rouet
...eurent au village de la...
...issa de saint léger de vi...
...ère Rouet son frère...

Left lower document

...la question de scavoir si
...la femme à la communauté
...lation de propos faitte par
...ue la femme puisse y succéder
...de leur enfant commun...
...e quand un mari seul stipul...
...ébité, meubles et effets mobil...
...aine soit et quil meurt
...enfant mineur, cet enfant
...e prélever cette soe sur
...propre de son pere, et
...propre pretend sa
...en cas quil viendroit
...decision à lieu soit que
...soit quelle ait renoncé
...mort de son mari, parceque
...es est antérieure à larcqn
...la conté, et que son
...méme de la durée de la
...olution d'icelle et qu'ainsi
...ne peut pas l'ancartir...
...de la renonciation de
...ecueille en même
...il reputé propre,
...la conté ensorte
...sur lui cette
...se par le creati...

Main right document (large calligraphy)

A Monsieur
Monsieur Le
Chatelain de la ville
De Besse ou Monsieur
votre Lieutenant

Supplie humblement
Jean Rahon Laboureur
habitant du village de
grouffaud paroisse de
picherande

Disant quil auroit

Etat des pieces de bois chaine
du bois de Castillon L'année

N° 1.

Prem.t une piece au vallon
du Leno Le chemin du vallon
...min du vallon...
...iculier Estime

Ensuitte au...
...Le chemin...
...Le chemin...

3.e janvier...
habits de deüil

V.e donataire
de certaine espece
de meubles et elle
contribuab.le aux
dettes
art. 214.

les Nottaires à Royan...
poitiers Soussignés ont comparu...
...Berland et...iselle Jeanne...
...ouse qui autorise...et de ce...
...eurants en cette ville...isé d...
...hospitallier,
la Solidairement et sous...
...us cy après aux 6.e jour d...
...u gré et volonté vendu ced...tence
...transporté vendent cedent...
...et transportent promettant qu...
...roubles hipoteques Eviction...
...ire et autres empechement...
...ment quelconque à peine de tou...
...dommages et interests,

Sieur Louis des coute...
...ourg de la Tranchée paroisse
triaize present Stipulant et acceptau.l
Luy les Sieurs ayants cause à l'avenir
est a Scavoir une maison Scituée
faux bourg de la tranchée Ditte
de St triaize consistant Lu vue
...tenant Lieu de Chambre basse
a costé, Deux Chambre haute
dessus ou jardin y attenaut
...Devant à La Rue ou Chemin...

By Tahir Shah

The Writer's Craft
The Reason to Write
Workbook: Comprehensive, Volume I & II
Workbook: Fantasy, Volume I & II
Workbook: Fiction, Volume I & II
Workbook: Historical Fiction, Volume I & II
Workbook: Teaching Stories, Volume I & II
Workbook: Travel, Volume I & II

Travel
Trail of Feathers
Travels With Myself
Beyond the Devil's Teeth
In Search of King Solomon's Mines
House of the Tiger King
In Arabian Nights
The Caliph's House
Sorcerer's Apprentice
Journey Through Namibia

Novels
Jinn Hunter: Book One – The Prism
Jinn Hunter: Book Two – The Jinnslayer
Jinn Hunter: Book Three – The Perplexity
Hannibal Fogg and the Supreme Secret of Man
Casablanca Blues
Eye Spy
Godman
Paris Syndrome
Timbuctoo

Anthologies
The Anthologies: Africa
The Anthologies: Ceremony
The Anthologies: Childhood
The Anthologies: City
The Anthologies: Danger
The Anthologies: East
The Anthologies: Expedition
The Anthologies: Frontier
The Anthologies: Hinterland
The Anthologies: India
The Anthologies: Jinns
The Anthologies: Jungle
The Anthologies: Magic
The Anthologies: Morocco
The Anthologies: Nasrudin
The Anthologies: People
The Anthologies: Quest
The Anthologies: South
The Anthologies: Taboo
The Anthologies: Teaching Stories
The Clockmaker's Box
The Tahir Shah Fiction Reader
The Tahir Shah Travel Reader

Edited by
Congress With a Crocodile
A Son of a Son, Volume I
A Son of a Son, Volume II

Research
Cultural Research
The Middle East Bedside Book
Three Essays

Nasrudin
Travels With Nasrudin
The Misadventures of the Mystifying Nasrudin
The Peregrinations of the Perplexing Nasrudin
The Voyages and Vicissitudes of Nasrudin
Nasrudin in the Land of Fools

Screenplays
Casablanca Blues: The Screenplay
Timbuctoo: The Screenplay

Teaching Stories
The Arabian Nights Adventures
Scorpion Soup
Tales Told to a Melon
The Afghan Notebook
Daydreams of an Octopus & Other Stories
The Caravanserai Stories
Ghoul Brothers
Hourglass
Imaginist
Jinn's Treasure
Jinnlore
Mellified Man
Skeleton Island
Wellspring
When the Sun Forgot to Rise
Outrunning the Reaper
The Cap of Invisibility
On Backgammon Time
The Wondrous Seed
The Paradise Tree
Mouse House
The Hoopoe's Flight
The Old Wind

A Treasury of Tales
The Tale of Double Six
The Forgotten Game
King of the Jinns
The Destiny Ring
Changing the World
A Tale of Witches
Cat, Mouse
Frogland
Mittle-Mittle
Capilongo
The Princess of Zilzilam
The Singing Serpents
The Tale of the Rusty Nail
The Unicorn's Tear
The Clockmaker Who Travelled Through Time
The Fish's Dream
The Man Whose Arms Grew Branches
The Most Foolish of Men
The Shop That Sold Truth
Qwerty
Renaissance
The Man With the Tiger's Head
The Kingdom of Blink
The Wisdom of Celestine
Dream Soup
The Skeleton Factory
An Unexpected Gift
The Problem Exchange
The Pharaoh Code
The Monkey Puzzle Club
Liquid Time
Cat Dog, Dog Cat
Princess Pickle's Laugh

THE REASON TO WRITE WORKBOOK:

FANTASY VOLUME I

TAHIR SHAH

THE REASON TO WRITE WORKBOOK:

FANTASY VOLUME I

TAHIR SHAH

MMXXV

Secretum Mundi Publishing Ltd.
124 City Road
London
EC1V 2NX
United Kingdom

www.secretum-mundi.com
info@secretum-mundi.com

First published by Secretum Mundi Publishing Ltd, 2025

THE REASON TO WRITE WORKBOOK:
FANTASY VOLUME I

VERSION 18012025

© TAHIR SHAH

Tahir Shah asserts the right to be identified as the Author of the Work
in accordance with the Copyright, Designs and Patents Act 1988.
A CIP catalogue record for this title is available from the British Library.

Visit the author's website at:

TahirShah.com

ISBN 978-1-915876-44-7

All rights reserved. No part of this publication may be reproduced, stored in a retrieval system, or transmitted, in any form or by any means, electronic, mechanical, photocopying, recording or otherwise, without the prior written permission of the publisher.

This book is sold subject to the condition that it shall not, by way of trade or otherwise, be lent, re-sold, hired out or otherwise circulated without the publisher's prior consent in any form of binding or cover other than that in which it is published and without a similar condition including this condition being imposed on the subsequent purchaser.

Contents

Introduction..1
A Note on Fantasy Writing...7
Using This Workbook..13
First Things First..17
Writing and You...21

ONE
Exercise 1..28
Exercise 2..30
Exercise 3..42
Exercise 4..46
Exercise 5..50

TWO
Exercise 6..60
Exercise 7..62
Exercise 8..66
Exercise 9..72
Exercise 10..76

THREE
Exercise 11..84
Exercise 12..86
Exercise 13..90
Exercise 14..94
Exercise 15..98

FOUR
Exercise 16..106
Exercise 17..108
Exercise 18..112
Exercise 19..114
Exercise 20..115

FIVE
Exercise 21..120
Exercise 22..122
Exercise 23..124
Exercise 24..126
Exercise 25..134

Writing Day: Beginning..139
Writing Day: Ending...143
The Notes..147

The fact that you are holding this book in your hands tells me that you're a writer.

You may not see yourself as one… not yet… but you are.

Believe in it, *really believe*, and you're going to find yourself embarking on the most incredible and unexpected journey of your life.

First, there's something I'd like you to do…

If you're sitting down, get out of the chair and go into your bathroom. Switch on the light, go over to the mirror, and look at yourself.

Don't look at your hair, brow, cheeks, or chin.

Look at your eyes.

Or, rather, look into your eyes.

Push your face up close so you see them and nothing else.

Stare into them, and into your soul.

While you're staring, greet yourself, calm yourself, and say the following words out loud:

**I am a writer.
I can feel it in my bones.
I am ready to embark on the greatest adventure of my life.**

I began my journey as a writer thirty years ago, and have come a long way since I stood in front of the bathroom mirror and stared at myself in the way I have just asked you to do.

In that time, I've experienced all manner of highs and lows.

Three things have been more important to me than anything else:

**The first: to only write for myself.
The second: never to listen to anyone who holds me back.
The third: to keep going, no matter what.**

Every week I receive dozens of messages from people who want to write books.

They rant on how it's their passion, how they've tried to get started, or how their friends and family ridicule them.

In my book *The Reason to Write: An Author's Masterclass*, I set out almost everything I could think of about my own writing journey. As anyone who has read it will know, the three tips I've just given here again are what I live by.

The thing about writing is that most people need to learn it. As I see it, learning to write is similar to building up muscle. Some people are fortunate to be born with an impressive physique, just as some people can write expertly from the get-go. But most people – me very much included – need to build up the muscle, so they go to the gym.

This series of books is a gymnasium for writers.

It's designed to build up muscle, and to get you in shape so that you can sit down and write the work you've always dreamt of putting out. All I'm going to do is show you how to do it, just as a trainer at a gym demonstrates how best to use the equipment.

The important thing is not to overthink.

Just as you do your reps at the gym without constantly worrying whether you're getting fitter or bigger, the same is true for the writer's path. The best progress is made when you devote yourself to the task at hand.

If you spend all your time caught up in a web of worry, you won't have the stamina needed to push ahead.

If you have already tackled any of the other workbooks in the series, you'll see that they've been constructed on rock-solid lines of continuity. There's lots of repetition, and plenty of exercises that may have you groaning out loud.

Believe me, repetition – and even groaning out loud – are good things, because they provide the one thing that makes a novice writer into a professional…

EXPERIENCE

In my life as an author, I have turned my hand to all kinds of genres and work. In that time, I've defied the established norms. As a result, I have been fortunate to be able to publish the work I wanted.

This is a subject that I covered in detail in *The Reason to Write*, and so I won't go over it again just yet. Suffice to say, I am an ardent believer in writers writing what they are destined to produce, rather than work that an agent, a publisher, or anyone else suggests.

Almost all the books on writing I have on my shelves were commissioned by publishers who grasped something certain – that they could make loads of cold hard cash by getting a hack writer to churn them out.

As a result, they sing to the standard model – one that glorifies agents and publishers, and belittles the author. The books in my series *The Reason to Write* are quite different.

They're all about YOU, and are about no one else.

I'm happy for you if you have family and friends who support you. But at the same time, my belief is that this is about you, and you alone. The danger of listening to the opinions of people who end up holding you back is so great that I believe you'll do best by going it alone.

As I say, I have written many kinds of work – including travel, fantasy, and journalism, fiction and non-fiction, short stories, screenplays, books for children, and a great deal else.

This workbook is concerned with fiction, and contains lessons learnt through writing numerous novels and fictional stories – work that sucked me into a twilight zone of wonder. The last thing of interest to me is whether the work is of interest to others.

What matters is that the journey of creation has changed me.

As with each workbook in the series, I have constructed it around work I have written myself, and on lessons that have preoccupied me along the way. The fact that I have published work in the genres discussed gives me an understanding into the writing involved at a granular level.

In the same way you would only trust a weaver to teach you to weave carpets if they had hands-on experience in the field, my sense is that the same is true for writing. Only an author who has considerable expertise in the genre concerned can hope to pass on what they know.

As you work your way through this book, focus on the exercise at hand, and forget about the bigger picture. Do the exercises with the care and attention they deserve, and do them because you're ready to progress, rather than because you're trying to impress others.

As anyone who knows me will attest, I rarely talk about work in progress, and never show anything until it's ready to be launched.

The last thing to remember once again is that you are a writer, just as there's a finished sculpture waiting in the lump of stone at the workshop of a great stone mason.

Trust in yourself.

Don't question.

Close your eyes and take a deep breath.

Sense the excitement permeating through every cell.

Now, let's make a start!

Tahir Shah

The way I see it, we come into the world with the inability to discern between fact and fantasy.

More importantly, we arrive here not needing, or wishing, to reference what is 'real' and what is not. The insatiable yearning to differentiate is the preserve of conditioning within certain cultures – and is something that was of no interest to our ancestors.

Through my travels in all corners of the world, I've learnt that what Occidental civilization so likes to chalk down as 'fantasy' is in actual fact regarded as reality by great swathes of the contemporary world.

I am constantly surprised at how society craves the fantastical as though it were a drug – ingesting it through books, movies, video games and the like – while encircling it carefully with a cordon... so that, at all times, everyone recognizes that it's fantasy.

Studies on electrical activity in the brain show that when we are exposed to the fantastical, it's like a Christmas tree being illuminated. My own thinking is that we are hard-wired to be exposed to the fantastical, and that when ideas or information are presented within an imaginary framework, we devour them.

My reasoning is that this was surely understood by our forebears, who used the fantastical as a way to embed key thinking that might guarantee the preservation of a people.

The result, of course, is mythology... and so much more.

This is the point at which some Western readers might start rolling their eyes. For, the way I perceive it, fantasy ought to be woven into the world around us at every level.

To understand what I mean, all you have to do is to look at children. In their reality, there's no differentiation between fact and fantasy.

When I was a kid, there were most definitely monsters under the bed.

In my wardrobe there was, without any question, an enchanted forest.

And I knew for certain that, if I could only climb up to the mirror above the bathroom sink, I'd be able to slip through into a magical realm.

That, my friends, is the default setting of humanity, and it's how we are supposed to be.

FANTASY VOLUME I

I'm giving you this spiel now because it shapes the subject we are here to discuss – fantasy. And, more importantly, literary fantasy.

How to think it.

How to live it.

And how to write it.

Writing fantasy is different from travel, or fiction, or even writing short stories.

My sense is that, in order to conjure the realms that are within you, you must recalibrate yourself first. You have to swim back through the waters of your imagination to a time when you, too, had monsters under the bed.

The good news is that, just as a total belief in the fantastical was born within you, it's still inside you. I've never met anyone – not even fact-loving scientists – who were incapable of remembering another time…

A time that made sense all because it was so nonsensical.

The fantastic may be alluring because we imagine it to be at odds with the world around us, but my thinking is that fantasy and the fantastical are hard-wired into us all.

We may be living lives of drudgery, yearning for escape, but that 'reality' is of little consequence, at least to our churning minds.

You don't need me to tell you that your dreams – if you remember them – are tinged with magic of every kind. If you stop to reflect for an instant, you'll see that your waking life is no less fantabulous.

Pause, let your mind wander, and the bedrock of normality around you will warp and mutate into the fantastical.

Humans are engines of fantasy, and we can't help but fantasize.

Indeed, the real challenge would be not to imagine wonders conjured from the very limits of impossibility. That means when you get down to writing fantasy, as you will, it's going to be a whole lot easier than you might imagine.

That is, it will be if you tap into the secret vortex of imagination that lies dormant in every cell. Trust it, love it, empower it, and it'll surge to life – as it's done in me, and in every writer applauded for their ability to mesmerize their readers with illusions made from nothing but words.

As with so many other genres of writing, strive not to overthink, to be someone you're not. Listen to the inner voices, channel them, and resist the need to channel the voices in another's head.

Your voices have been given to you for a reason – to tap like the milk from a rubber tree, and to provide in abundance to the world.

In my own experience, writing is a realm in which I lose myself, walking a tightrope above a great indomitable waterfall of sheering mania.

But it's fantasy writing that transports me over that tightrope at warp speed, my feet moving with such rapidity that they're blurred, and my head so awed by the experience that it's fogged with delicious ecstasy.

As you embark on this workbook, my great hope is that you'll embrace the experience and push the boundaries, allowing yourself to channel the voices that are whispering to you, begging to be set free from the limits of your own imagination.

As I've already said, this workbook is about you and your journey as a writer.

It's not about proving yourself to anyone else. Nor is it about getting through it fast so that you can rush ahead to another workbook in the series.

In truth, the very best way to tackle it would be to start all over again once you have finished, and then again after that. But I'm not a sadist, and I want you to get on with your own writing projects – because that's what matters most.

Please remember that in the exercises there are no perfect answers. If possible, apply yourself to every question, and never allow yourself to complete any of the questions on 'autopilot'.

It's up to you whether you write your answers in the physical book or type them on an electronic device. What matters is that you treat each exercise as though it's an individual workout at the gym.

Ideally, it would be best to make it all the way to the end of an exercise before you take a break. Just as with the gym, you may still have energy to keep going. If you do, my suggestion is to stop once you're done, rather than getting to the point of exhaustion.

This workbook is about challenging you as a writer, and overcoming the various hurdles that are common to us all.

For example, one of the hardest things about writing is getting started – so if the thought of getting back to the workbook is exhilarating, you'll do so much better than if it feels like a chore.

For years, I used to have a little yellow Post-it note on the wall above my desk. On it, I'd scribbled something that has always held me in good stead:

Do work you're in the mood for!

Most of the time I only write when I am in the mood for it – which is good because I so often am. But I am because I allow the magic of writing to enthuse me, and to seep into every cell and into the marrow of my bones.

If the thought of spending an hour or two with this workbook is exhilarating to you, it would fill me with unbridled delight.

In a moment we're going to dive in at the deep end, but I promise we will start easy and will take it slow. The important thing is that you promise me something – that you'll devote the same amount of time to this workbook each day.

You may only have twenty minutes a day. If that's all you have, don't stress. That'll be fine. The key thing is that you try and turn to the workbook at the same time each day and, if possible, under the same conditions.

A central point for a successful writer is routine.

Build up the routine and you'll build up the muscle. In my experience, a good routine eases you into the day's work, and turns it from a chore to a pleasure.

The next thing to do is to look at the place where you'll be doing the exercises. Feel comfortable there. Feel calm. Feel happy. Best not to have your phone buzzing with messages or notifications. As a writer, you're going to need to learn to get into the zone, and the best way to do that is by building a shrine…

The desk on which you are working is a shrine – not a religious shrine so much as a literary one. Your shrine is connected to all the writers in history who have sat down to accomplish a literary feat. They all share one thing in common: the fact that, at one time, they had never written a single line or published anything at all.

None of them reached their ambitions until they'd built up literary muscle, just as you're going to do.

Being a successful writer will require you to tap into something invisible, something that's deep inside you. I don't even know what to call it, so I'll call it the 'inner force of creation'. It's in us all. Some people find it easier than others to tap into. The reason they're so good at rooting it out amid all the random thoughts, the memories, and the angst is because they have learned to channel it. Or because experience in life gave them a way to access it.

Think of it like a well in a remote village.

The people living there may be uncertain whether there's water under the ground. So they dig and they dig, and they dig and they dig, and eventually they reach the water table. It's delicious fresh water, and they're all thrilled to bits.

Now that they have the shaft, they don't have to dig down each time they want to get to the water. Instead, they just tug the cover away, lower down a bucket, and take what they need.

Writing is exactly the same.

Once you have dug down to the well, you can get to the water whenever you need. All you have to do is to protect the well, and to make sure that it stays clean. Look after the well, and the precious reserve of water inside, and it'll look after you.

Now, take another deep breath, because it's time to focus.

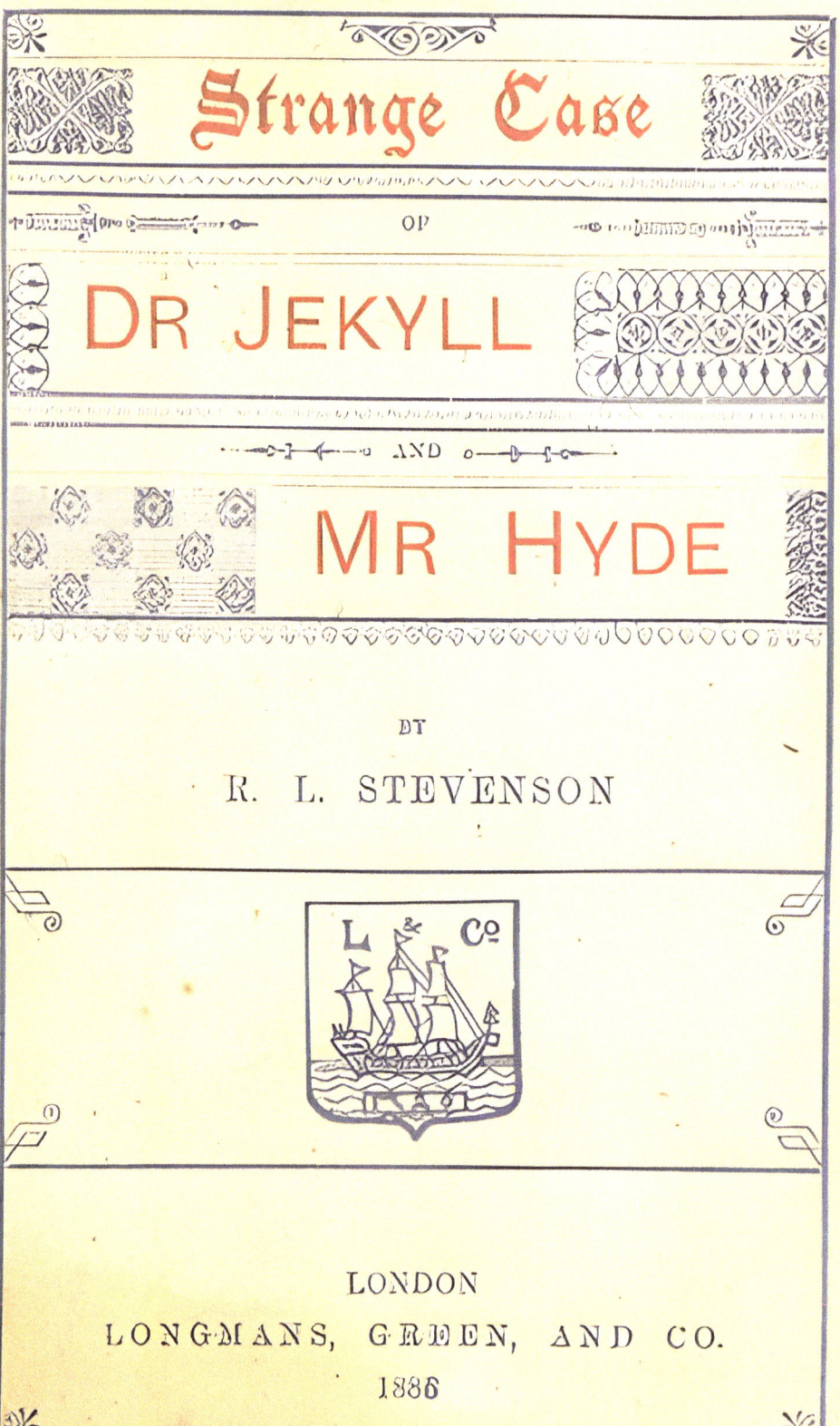

THE HOBBIT

or
There and Back
Again

BY

J. R. R. TOLKIEN

ILLUSTRATIONS BY
THE AUTHOR

BOSTON AND NEW YORK
HOUGHTON MIFFLIN COMPANY
1938

In the space that follows, write about yourself and why you want to write. This needs to come from the inner you, and not from the you who's fearful of what others think. They say that you should dance as though no one is watching. Do this exercise with the same feeling – that it's about you and no one else. Be honest but, more importantly, be ambitious and be brave. Again, believe in yourself.

In the space below, detail what writing means to you. Explain to yourself why this genre is important and give details of any events or experiences in your life that made you want to write.

Jinn Hunter

Book Two

The Jinnslayer

Tahir Shah

NIGHT

A FANTASY

by

LOWELL S. HALE

PETER G. BOYLE   :-:   *Publisher*
267-275 West 17th Street   New York City

EXERCISE 1

Read the following text, then close your eyes for a full minute and allow a scene to appear. When you are ready, complete the exercise below.

Poised in the corner of his octagonal cell, Nequissimus slipped into an insentient state – a state known to the malbino guards as moöl.

Glowing in putrid grey-green, his slippery scales shimmering like algae on the Ocean of Fecund Fear, the great jinn closed his many eyes and began to brood. He was considering the terror he would wreak on escaping, and of the pathetic frailty of the malbinos who guarded him.

As he brooded, he began to tremble ever so slightly.

A trembling that grew, fragment on fragment, until the octagonal cubicle's floor and walls were vibrating. The captive jinn in the cells above might have protested, but none dared. They knew full well Nequissimus could snuff out their lives, or drive them to raw insanity with a single whisper – a whisper hissed in the blink of an unblinking eye.

However mighty, no creature was protected from the murmurs of Nequissimus.

No one except for the malbinos.

For three days and nights, the trembling went on.

With each moment, it grew in pitch and volume, until the entire Prism was vibrating. Every last sheet of impenetrable glass was shuddering and grinding, swaying back and forth, the cells ringing with the crazed screeching clatter of fear.

From: *Jinn Hunter: Book One – The Prism*

In your own time, write a description of what you saw when your eyes were closed.

If you find yourself deviating from the scene you imagined, go with it, and write anything you like.

The important thing is that, if possible, you should try and keep writing without stopping.

Write as much or as little as you like.

You can either write in note form, or in a more polished style.

Remember, no one is going to read what you write, so no one will judge you.

Indeed, it's better if you don't reread the text you write, at least not for now.

EXERCISE 2

In the space below, write the names of six authors of fantasy whose writing has inspired you.

1
2
3
4
5
6

In the space below, list six works of fantasy by an author whose work you know well.

1
2
3
4
5
6

In the space below, write six descriptive words to describe fantasy writing.

1.
2.
3.
4.
5.
6.

In the space below, list six reasons why the fantasy genre appeals to you.

1.
2.
3.
4.
5.
6.

In the space below, write a sentence describing four types of fantastical vehicle of any kind.

1

2

3

4

In the space below, write as many words as you can that are synonyms for the word given:

Magical

Fanciful

Peculiar

Spellbound

In the space below, write a paragraph describing an ant meeting a hedgehog at a railway station.

In the space below, write a paragraph about a message being found in a corked bottle by a scarlet macaw.

In the space below, write six descriptive words to describe a fairy.

1
2
3
4
5
6

In the space below, write six descriptive words to describe the fairy's wings.

1
2
3
4
5
6

In the space below, write six descriptive words to describe the fairy's smile.

1.
2.
3.
4.
5.
6.

In the space below, write six descriptive words to describe the place where the fairy lives.

1.
2.
3.
4.
5.
6.

In the space below, write four sentences describing a fairy's secret dreams.

1

2

3

4

In the space below, write as many words as you can that are synonyms for the word given:

Expressive

Prudish

Lethargic

Brief

In the space below, write a paragraph describing an eagle turned into a human troll by a sorceress.

In the space below, write a paragraph describing a shipwreck kingdom at the bottom of the Jade Sea.

In the space below, write six descriptive words to describe imagination.

1
2
3
4
5
6

In the space below, write six descriptive words to describe poison.

1
2
3
4
5
6

In the space below, write six descriptive words to describe a treasure cave.

1
2
3
4
5
6

In the space below, write six descriptive words to describe fear.

1
2
3
4
5
6

In the space below, write four sentences to describe the ancestors of a goblin king.

1

2

3

4

In the space below, write as many words as you can that are synonyms for the word given:

Rude

Hideous

Bountiful

Wretched

In the space below, write a paragraph describing a land lost in cloud.

In the space below, write a paragraph about a kingdom of the blind, in which a one-eyed man is king.

EXERCISE 3

In the space below, write six descriptive words to describe a toothbrush that has come to life.

1
2
3
4
5
6

In the space below, write six descriptive words to describe an oak leaf that dreams to be an emperor.

1
2
3
4
5
6

In the space below, write six descriptive words to describe a cat that fears its shadow.

1.
2.
3.
4.
5.
6.

In the space below, write six descriptive words to describe cold.

1.
2.
3.
4.
5.
6.

In the space below, write four sentences about lost hope.

1

2

3

4

In the space below, write as many words as you can that are synonyms for the word given:

Long

Stern

Bleak

Jubilant

In the space below, write a paragraph describing a potion that provides a sixth sense.

In the space below, write a paragraph about a dog with three human heads.

EXERCISE 4

In the space below, write six descriptive words to describe a cowardly hero.

1
2
3
4
5
6

In the space below, write six descriptive words to describe thunder.

1
2
3
4
5
6

In the space below, write six descriptive words to describe the sound of torrential rain.

1
2
3
4
5
6

In the space below, write six descriptive words to describe splendour.

1
2
3
4
5
6

In the space below, write four sentences to describe a fruit market from a fantasy kingdom.

1

2

3

4

In the space below, write as many words as you can that are synonyms for the word given:

Packet

Bottle

Bird

Fortress

In the space below, write a paragraph describing a box containing an entire kingdom of fleas.

In the space below, write a paragraph about an otter that has fallen in love with a rattlesnake.

EXERCISE 5

In the space below, write six descriptive words to describe imaginary life forms you yourself have thought up.

1
2
3
4
5
6

In the space below, write six descriptive words to describe a fantastical wedding.

1
2
3
4
5
6

In the space below, write six descriptive words to describe uninvited guests at the wedding.

1
2
3
4
5
6

In the space below, write six descriptive words to describe embarrassment.

1
2
3
4
5
6

In the space below, write four sentences to describe the terror of the wind.

1

2

3

4

In the space below, write as many words as you can that are synonyms for the word given:

Adorned

Enlightened

Chaste

Uneven

In the space below, write a paragraph describing a battle between two ogres.

In the space below, write a paragraph about an ogre with a remarkable secret.

NOTES

(144)

his eyes were like disks of blue fire.
He was trembling all over.
"Dorian!" he began.
"Don't speak."
"But what is the matter? Of course
I won't look at it if you don't
want me to," he said rather
coldly, turning on his heel, and
going over towards the window. "But
really it seems rather absurd that
I shouldn't see my own work, especially
as I am going to exhibit it in
Paris, in the autumn. I shall
probably have to give it another
coat of varnish before that, so I
must see it someday, and why
not today?"
"To exhibit it! You want to
exhibit it?" exclaimed Dorian Grey,
with a strange sense of horror
creeping over him. Was the world
going to be shown his secret? Were
people to gape at the mystery of
his life? that was impossible.
Something, he did not know what,
had to be done at once.
"Yes, I don't suppose you will
object to that. Georges Petit is
going to collect all my best
pictures for a special exhibition
in the Rue de Sèze, which will
open the first week in October.

EXERCISE 6

Read the following text, then close your eyes for a full minute and allow a scene to appear. When you are ready, complete the exercise below.

For three horizons, Amar the admiral spoke of his life, but never once did he mention the sea.

Plodding alongside his travelling companion, listening intently to the stream of tales, Borbor pined for solitude. Far too well-mannered to regale the admiral with a story of his own from the caravanserai of Mishmak, he listened…

… and listened, wishing he was alone.

The great Crushed Glass Desert eventually came to an end, replaced by a wide dominion called Xöx, where the days and nights were no more than ten minutes long. The landscape was abundantly fertile, and the people who farmed it were overly kind.

Inviting the travellers into their homes, they plied them with food and friendship in equal measure. Meals tended to run into each other in Xöx, in a long and constant stream of dining. Breakfast became dinner, and dinner became breakfast, and both were a reason to tell portions of a grand tapestry, the epic Tale of the Three Clouds.

It was all that mattered to the people of Xöx.

A tale so important that it was studied as though it were a religious scripture, cherished by every man, woman, and child. A tale so long, and so intertwined, that there was never any chance at all of anyone ever entertaining a guest with the same passage twice. As it was of such epic length, it took an entire lifetime to commit the full tale to memory.

From: *Jinn Hunter: Book Two – The Jinnslayer*

In your own time, write a description of what you saw when your eyes were closed.

If you find yourself deviating from the scene you imagined, go with it – and write anything you like.

The important thing is that, if possible, you should try and keep writing without stopping.

Write as much or as little as you like.

You can either write in note form, or in a more polished style.

Remember, no one is going to read what you write, so no one will judge you.

Indeed, it's better if you don't reread the text you write, at least not for now.

EXERCISE 7

In the space below, name six different fantastical or imaginary dwellings.

1

2

3

4

5

6

In the space below, write a short description of each of the dwellings.

1

2

3

4

5

6

In the space below, write the name of six kinds of people, creatures, or life forms who live in the dwellings.

1

2

3

4

5

6

In the space below, write a short description of each kind of person, creature, or life form you listed above.

1

2

3

4

5

6

In the space below, write a paragraph describing the groups of people or creatures, providing as much detail as you can of their values and their society.

In the space below, write a paragraph explaining a major event that took place within their history, and which shaped their society.

EXERCISE 8

In the space below, write the names of six types of landscape in which a fantasy story or novel might take place. These can be actual landscapes, or imaginary or fantastical ones.

1

2

3

4

5

6

In the space below, write a short description of each of the different landscapes you have listed above. Try to provide unusual details about them.

1

2

3

4

5

6

In the space below, write a short description of people or creatures who inhabit the landscapes, but which would rarely be mentioned in a story or book.

1

2

3

4

5

6

In the space below, write a description of what lies beneath each landscape, or above it – or both. Again, try to think out of the box, and be creative.

1

2

3

4

5

6

FANTASY VOLUME I

In the space below, write four sentences describing heroes from a fantastical realm.

1

2

3

4

In the space below, write as many words as you can that are synonyms for the word given:

Imagination

Fascinate

Discover

Infinity

In the space below, write a paragraph describing a fantastical or imaginary character sitting on a park bench, and what is going through their mind.

In the space below, write a paragraph of the fantastical or imaginary character from above meeting another character. The two characters can be utterly different if you like, taken from two entirely different lines of imagination.

EXERCISE 9

In the space below, write two sentences imagining a secret tunnel.

In the space below, write two sentences imagining a treasure vault within a mountain.

In the space below, write two sentences that describe a guardian of the treasure vault described above.

In the space below, write two sentences that describe someone or something that is set on stealing the treasure.

In the space below, write four sentences to describe how the treasure got to where it is, what is contained there, a secret about it, and what is about to take place.

1

2

3

4

In the space below, write as many words that describe the following:

An ogre

A genie or jinn

A phantom

A warlock

In the space below, write a paragraph describing a market on a distant planet, in which all manner of wares are on sale. Free your imagination, and be as descriptive as possible.

In the space below, write a paragraph about one of the traders in the market described above. Tell us what they sell, what goes through their mind, and what their plan is for getting revenge on their sworn enemy. Again, be as descriptive as possible.

EXERCISE 10

In the space below, write a pair of sentences that describe the clothing of a character from a fantasy story or book who can imagine writing.

In the space below, write a pair of sentences that describe the youth of that character.

In the space below, write a pair of sentences that describe a secret of that character.

In the space below, write a pair of sentences that describe someone learning about the secret.

FANTASY VOLUME I

In the space below, write four long sentences about people, creatures, or life forms known to the character you have been describing.

1

2

3

4

In the space below, write as many words as you can that are synonyms for the word given:

Myth

Enigma

Fantasy

Monster

In the space below, write a paragraph describing a fantastical creature that you yourself have imagined, layering it with as much detail as possible.

Take three or four details from your paragraph above, and expand them, providing yet more layers of detail.

The Fisherman

When I was young and foolish, but so certain I was wise, I took any work offered.

Sometimes I toiled days at a stretch without ever sleeping – cleaning fish, bailing water from flimsy craft, scrubbing filth from the decks. And at other times I would lose myself in strange lands, listen to the tales that sailors so like to tell, and would think of the love I had left a world away at home.

The years passed.

Look at my hands and you will see I tell you the truth. My palms are coarse and calloused, tattooed with adventure and with the trials of fate.

Frequently, I promised myself to quit the life of roaming, to settle down in Haifa, where my family was from. But each time I reached my own port, I was talked into embarking on yet one more journey.

And another.

Then, one night in the month of August, my fishing vessel was wrecked during a violent summer gale off the coast of North Africa. The only survivor, I was captured and taken prisoner by a band of Barbary pirates.

Nothing pleased them more than gaining another seaman for nothing, a lost soul to barter in the slave market at Oran.

They had in their party thirty others already. Each one a rough sea dog scraped up from Barbary shores; each of them just enough alive to coax a ransom.

EXERCISE 11

Read the following text, then close your eyes for a full minute and allow a scene to appear. When you are ready, complete the exercise below.

Fists clenched, Amalorous strode up to the doors of the Cadenta Hall, heaved open by the guards even before the leader's shadow had reached them.

As his feet crossed the threshold, the floor rinsed in blood, swelling up through the labyrinthine design.

Annis and Amarath sensed fear in their bones and, on their tongues, the taste of death.

At double speed Amalorous paced through the hall, his bare feet drenched in red. His expression frozen, and his fists still clenched tight in rage, he made a beeline for the casket.

Having reached it, he peered in at the gruesome remains, closed his eyes, and thought very hard.

A childhood memory slipped onto the stage of his mind.

Three boys whirling and swirling their homemade swords.

Cries of infantile battle.

An unexpected injury.

Anguish.

A remedy as startling as the wound itself.

From: *Jinn Hunter: Book Three – The Perplexity*

FANTASY VOLUME I

In your own time, write a description of what you saw when your eyes were closed.

If you find yourself deviating from the scene you imagined, go with it – and write anything you like.

The important thing is that, if possible, you should try and keep writing without stopping.

Write as much or as little as you like.

You can either write in note form, or in a more polished style.

Remember, no one is going to read what you write, so no one will judge you.

Indeed, it's better if you don't reread the text you write, at least not for now.

EXERCISE 12

In the space below, write a short description of a princess who's been turned into a moth.

In the space below, write a description of the inner thoughts of the moth-princess.

In the space below, write a description of the moth-princess's hopes for the future.

In the space below, write a description of the witch who turned the princess into a moth.

In the space below, write a description of an elixir that could turn the moth back into a princess.

In the space below, write a description of a prince the princess has seen while in the guise of the moth.

In the space below, write a description of the moth-princess's love for the prince.

In the space below, write a description of the kingdom to which the moth-princess belongs.

In the space below, write a paragraph of the moth-princess devising a plan to get the elixir and break the spell.

NOTES

EXERCISE 13

Use a reference source of your choice to complete this exercise.

Imagine a fantastical kingdom or realm, and make a list of ten imaginary people or creatures who live or have lived there, giving nine details from the lives of each one.

1 Name:

   Details:

i.   ii.   iii.

iv.   v.   vi.

vii.   viii.   ix.

2 Name:

   Details:

i.   ii.   iii.

iv.   v.   vi.

vii.   viii.   ix.

3   Name:

   Details:

i.   ii.   iii.

iv.   v.   vi.

vii.   viii.   ix.

4   Name:

   Details:

i.   ii.   iii.

iv.   v.   vi.

vii.   viii.   ix.

5   Name:

   Details:

i.   ii.   iii.

iv.   v.   vi.

vii.   viii.   ix.

6 Name:

   Details:

i.   ii.   iii.

iv.   v.   vi.

vii.   viii.   ix.

7 Name:

   Details:

i.   ii.   iii.

iv.   v.   vi.

vii.   viii.   ix.

8 Name:

   Details:

i.   ii.   iii.

iv.   v.   vi.

vii.   viii.   ix.

9   Name:

    Details:

i.   ii.   iii.

iv.   v.   vi.

vii.   viii.   ix.

10 Name:

    Details:

i.   ii.   iii.

iv.   v.   vi.

vii.   viii.   ix.

EXERCISE 14

Imagine multiple fantastical kingdoms or realms, and name each one. They do not need to be associated with each other in any way.

Kingdoms or realms

i. ii. iii.

iv. v. vi.

vii. viii. ix.

Now name:

Cities, towns, or villages there

i. ii. iii.

iv. v. vi.

vii. viii. ix.

Landmarks

i.   ii.   iii.

iv.   v.   vi.

vii.   viii.   ix.

Good people or creatures there

i.   ii.   iii.

iv.   v.   vi.

vii.   viii.   ix.

Evil people or creatures there

i.   ii.   iii.

iv.   v.   vi.

vii.   viii.   ix.

Types of food there

i.   ii.   iii.

iv.   v.   vi.

vii.   viii.   ix.

Works of poetry, music, writing, art, or sculpture

i.   ii.   iii.

iv.   v.   vi.

vii.   viii.   ix.

Details of the ruler

i.   ii.   iii.

iv.   v.   vi.

vii.   viii.   ix.

Details of enemies

i.   ii.   iii.

iv.   v.   vi.

vii.   viii.   ix.

The most wonderful things about the kingdom or realm

i.   ii.   iii.

iv.   v.   vi.

vii.   viii.   ix.

The very worst things about the kingdom or realm

i.   ii.   iii.

iv.   v.   vi.

vii.   viii.   ix.

EXERCISE 15

Think of a fantastical character from a fantasy novel or story you know well and describe them.

Describe the same character, imagining they were a warlock.

Describe the same character, imagining they were a magician.

Describe the same character, imagining they were a warrior.

Describe the same character, imagining they had been blessed with an astonishing skill.

Describe a second fantastical character, but one you have imagined.

Describe the character's strengths.

Describe their hidden weaknesses.

Compare the first fantastical character to the second.

Consider why the author of the novel or story created their character as they did.

NOTES

II

THE KING'S SON AND THE DERVISH'S DAUGHTER

Once upon a time there was a sea Captain who built a fine ship, manned her with many good sailors, and sailed in her from the White[1] to the Black Sea. But it so happened that the weather became stormy, and before they reached the haven for which they were bound their water fell short. So the Captain bade his men steer for the nearest shore, and presently they spied a little town and cast anchor before it. Lowering their boat, they placed some water-kegs in it, and rowed ashore. On the quay a number of boys were playing. Calling one of them to him, the Captain showed him a piastre, and said,

'Here, my lad, lead us to the fountain, and this coin is thine.'

Now, this boy was baldheaded; but as he seemed bright and clever, the Captain took a fancy to him, and when his men had got their

[1] The Ægean Sea.

EXERCISE 16

Read the following text, then close your eyes for a full minute and allow a scene to appear. When you are ready, complete the exercise below.

My father once told me that I was born during a tempest, the storm clouds darker grey than any other he had ever seen.

It may sound fanciful, but I have always imagined those brooding clouds were somehow born inside me as I took my first pained gasps of air.

The reason was that, throughout my childhood and much of my life, I was known by everyone as the 'Grey Man'.

I loved that colour, took solace in it, and liked having it as my name.

The other children would be dressed in vibrant colours, while I begged my mother to allow me wear grey. I would choose books to read which had grey covers, search out grey food, and to only used go out at twilight, when the city and the landscape was as grey as a pencil sketch.

The grey life suited me, for I was comforted by the one hue that appeared to be as fond of me as I was of it.

Once I had left school, I became an apprentice to a blacksmith. Working at the forge from morning till night, my face, arms, and hands were always as grey as the clothing I wore for the job.

From: *Imaginist*

In your own time, write a description of what you saw when your eyes were closed.

If you find yourself deviating from the scene you imagined, go with it – and write anything you like.

The important thing is that, if possible, you should try and keep writing without stopping.

Write as much or as little as you like.

You can either write in note form, or in a more polished style.

Remember, no one is going to read what you write, so no one will judge you.

Indeed, it's better if you don't reread the text you write, at least not for now.

EXERCISE 17

Imagine a dinner party at which there are eight imaginary or fantastical guests seated around a table. Each one is very different from the others. Detail for each guest their great obsession, weakness, fear, wish, and secret.

Guest 1

Obsession

Weakness

Fear

Wish

Secret

Guest 2

Obsession

Weakness

Fear

Wish

Secret

Guest 3

Obsession

Weakness

Fear

Wish

Secret

Guest 4

Obsession

Weakness

Fear

Wish

Secret

Guest 5

Obsession

Weakness

Fear

Wish

Secret

Guest 6

Obsession

Weakness

Fear

Wish

Secret

Guest 7

Obsession

Weakness

Fear

Wish

Secret

Guest 8

Obsession

Weakness

Fear

Wish

Secret

NOTES

EXERCISE 18

Imagine you are in a fantastical kingdom or realm, and that you are reading a newspaper there. In the space provided, detail five events that are described on the front page of the newspaper.

Event 1

Event 2

Event 3

Event 4

Event 5

EXERCISE 19

Take one of the news stories listed above and describe it in a fuller way, providing as much detail as possible about the people, characters, or life forms involved.

EXERCISE 20

In the space below, write a letter from the main protagonist mentioned in the news story above, to anyone else. If possible, use the letter to comment on the news story, i.e., as seen from the inside track.

THE RETURN OF THE KING

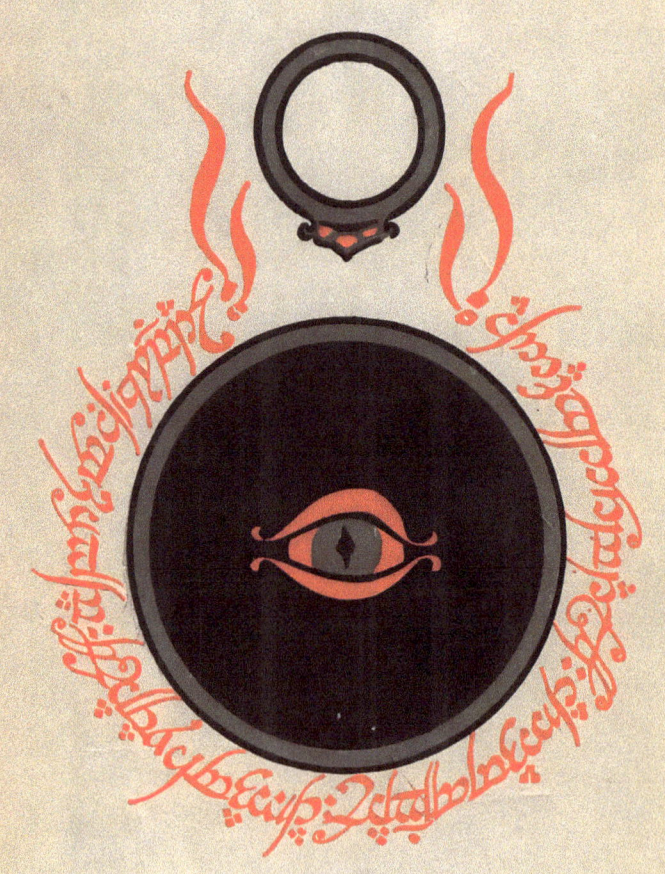

J. R. R. TOLKIEN

THROUGH THE LOOKING-GLASS.

who liked being very exact, had argued that they couldn't, because there were only two of them, and Alice had been reduced at last to say "Well, *you* can be one of them then, and *I'll* be all the rest." And once she had really frightened her old nurse by shouting suddenly

in her ear, "Nurse! Do let's pretend that I'm a hungry hyæna, and you're a bone!"

But this is taking us away from Alice's speech to the kitten. "Let's pretend that you're the Red Queen, Kitty! Do you know, I think, if you sat up and folded your arms, you'd look exactly like her. Now do try, there's a dear!" And Alice got the Red Queen off the table, and set it up before the kitten as a model for it to imitate: however, the thing didn't succeed, principally, Alice said, because the kitten wouldn't fold its arms properly. So, to punish it, she held it

EXERCISE 21

Read the following text, then close your eyes for a full minute and allow a scene to appear. When you are ready, complete the exercise below.

By the third horizon, Borbor's feet were numb from walking, his shoulders aching, the underripe mandigo yam having turned to mush.

Trudging forwards, his mind lost in self-pity, he did his best to imagine being back serving smorop pods at the Mishmak Lodge. His employer, Mr. Ot, may have been a slave driver, but Borbor missed the job, and the regular clientele.

Most of all, he missed the smorop pods – the one fruit he couldn't bear to eat.

As he plodded on and on, Mr. Ot's face glided into his mind with increasing frequency.

Each time, it boomed the same furious message:

'Use your jinn powers to get back right away, you imbecile!'

As Borbor had struggled to inform the fugitive Jinn Hunter in the Kingdom of Imagined Souls, he'd pledged not to use his powers.

Bouncing thoughts turning to the fugitive, he wondered for a moment what could have become of him.

The thought was chased from his daydream as swiftly as it had arrived.

Chased out by the sound of mechanical legs.

The lemon-yellow jinn spun round.

Heading across the barren plain at colossal speed was an animal-shaped machine. Headless, the extended bulk was crafted from burnished brass and bore sixteen legs and feet, arranged in groups of four on nimble hooves.

Riding it, like a jockey hurtling a steed down the final stretch, was a dog jinn.

As it approached the traveller, the creature reared up, its eccentric form catching the sun. Reined in by its master, it came to a halt in Borbor's shadow.

From: *Jinn Hunter: Book Three – The Perplexity*

In your own time, write a description of what you saw when your eyes were closed.

If you find yourself deviating from the scene you imagined, go with it – and write anything you like.

The important thing is that, if possible, you should try and keep writing without stopping.

Write as much or as little as you like.

You can either write in note form, or in a more polished style.

Remember, no one is going to read what you write, so no one will judge you.

Indeed, it's better if you don't reread the text you write, at least not for now.

EXERCISE 22

Consider that you are sustaining an attack of any kind in an imaginary kingdom or realm. Write a description, providing as much detail as possible.

FANTASY VOLUME I

EXERCISE 23

Rewrite the description of the attack from the previous exercise as though it were written in a newspaper in the third person.

FANTASY VOLUME I

EXERCISE 24

Write a succinct journal entry for a warlock with depression.

Write a succinct journal entry for an ogre who has just fallen in love.

Write a succinct journal entry for a warrior about to go to battle.

Write a succinct journal entry for an explorer on a doomed adventure.

Write a succinct journal entry for a jinn that guards a treasure vault.

Write a succinct journal entry for a fairytale character of your choosing.

Write a succinct journal entry for a wizard who has lost faith in life.

Write a succinct journal entry for the rider of a magic horse.

In the space below, write short descriptions of three characters for a fantasy novel or story.

1

2

3

In bulletpoint form, plan out the story arc of a fantasy novel or story.

FANTASY VOLUME I

In the space below, write three versions of a first sentence of the fantasy story or book you have planned out above.

1

2

3

In the space below, take the best first sentence and expand it into a first paragraph.

Now, in the space below, continue writing the first paragraph, and write the first page of the fantasy novel or story.

EXERCISE 25

Imagine a fictitious pop musician and complete a detailed biography for them, giving as many details as possible, such as names of their releases, awards, and information about their failures as well as their triumphs.

Name

Dates

Education and early life

Career

Personal life

Charity work

Influences

Musical releases

Awards

Scandals

Legacy

PETER PAN
IN
KENSINGTON
GARDENS
BY J. M. BARRIE

ILLUSTRATED BY ARTHUR RACKHAM

HODDER & STOUGHTON, LIMITED, PUBLISHERS, LONDON

Aükelé
and the Water-of-Life

IN THE ancient days, my little brothers and sisters, when our ancestors lived in the land to the west that we call Helani-the-Distant, the Land-that-Supports-the-Heavens—before they first came to this rainbowed Hawaii—there was a High-Chief of that country named Iku, who had eleven sons, and the youngest was so much handsomer and cleverer than the others that he was his father's favourite.

He was loved best of all, too, by his grandmother, who watched over his babyhood, an old woman so old that she remembered the time when the trees talked together, with skin rugged and blackened like a lizard's, hair the colour of ashes, and eyes as red as fire-coals. She was a Sorceress, who went

One could resort to all kinds of metaphors and clichés to describe writing a book.

It's not a sprint but a marathon.

Rather like marathon running, you must have your head in the right zone – because if you aren't thinking straight, you'll flounder.

For me, the key way to think straight is to pace myself from the start, and to have my eyes trained firmly on the finish line – or, better, well beyond it.

As I have ranted on elsewhere, go into it without obsessive self-examining. Keep focused on the new few feet of road, keep writing, and the manuscript will be completed in no time.

Imagine the finished work sitting on your mantelpiece.

Feel proud about it.

Allow the sense of being a published author to wash over you.

By planning the project well, and by using the muscle you've built up through the exercises of this workbook, you *will* reach the finish line.

That's certainty.

In order to conserve your energy, and to have the stamina you'll need, I suggest you don't tell too many family members and friends about what you're doing. Imagine their amazement at seeing you have written and published a book, and that they hadn't known about it.

Another apt metaphor for book writing is that of a plant growing from a seed. First, you plant the tiny seed and coax it to develop into a sapling. Then, as you tend it, giving it water and sunshine, it grows and grows and takes on a life force of itself.

As you set out on the journey of writing the manuscript, remember that you have the tools to complete the adventure.

But fix in your mind the point that if you question your ability or the work you have done, you're sliding back down as though in a game of literary snakes and ladders.

Although it may seem off-beat, the following exercise is likely to help with setting the stage.

Create a writing ritual for yourself, and know deep down that when you have done the ritual before you start, you are absolutely ready – and that the work you'll be doing will be fantabulous because the ritual has been done.

It's up to you what the ritual will be like, whether it'll be simple or elaborate. Of course, it's perfectly fine to start simple and make it more elaborate as you go on.

Here, for instance, is a writing ritual I have used for the last two or three books I've written at the desk I'm sitting at:

- Clean my reading glasses thoroughly, fold the lens cloth and place it to the left of my screen.

- Pick up the 'wishing stone' my favourite aunt gave me and touch it to my cheek.

- Line up my pens and pencils.

- Close my eyes and think of the garden at my childhood home.

- Reach for the bottle of 'writing cologne' (see Cologne in The Notes section), dab a little on the back of my right hand, and breathe it in.

- Read through the previous day's work.

- Touch the wishing stone again.

- And begin…

In the space below, note down a writing ritual bullet-point form.

-

-

-

-

-

-

-

Chapter 1

THE TAMING OF SMÉAGOL

'Well, master, we're in a fix and no mistake,' said Sam Gamgee. He stood despondently with hunched shoulders beside Frodo, and peered out with puckered eyes into the gloom.

It was the third evening since they had fled from the Company, as far as they could tell: they had almost lost count of the hours during which they had climbed and laboured among the barren slopes and stones of the Emyn Muil, sometimes retracing their steps because they could find no way forward, sometimes discovering that they had wandered in a circle back to where they had been hours before. Yet on the whole they had worked steadily eastward, keeping as near as they could find a way to the outer edge of this strange twisted knot of hills. But always they found its outward faces sheer, high and impassable, frowning over the plain below; beyond its tumbled skirts lay livid festering marshes where nothing moved and not even a bird was to be seen.

The hobbits stood now on the brink of a tall cliff, bare and bleak, its feet wrapped in mist; and behind them rose the broken highlands crowned with drifting cloud. A chill wind blew from the East. Night was gathering over the shapeless lands before them; the sickly green of them was fading to a sullen brown. Far away to the right the Anduin, that had gleamed fitfully in sun-breaks during the day, was now hidden in shadow. But their eyes did not look beyond the River, back to Gondor, to their friends, to the lands of Men. South and east they stared to where, at the edge of the oncoming night, a dark line hung, like distant mountains of motionless smoke. Every now and again a tiny red gleam far away flickered upwards on the rim of earth and sky.

'What a fix!' said Sam. 'That's the one place in all the lands we've ever heard of that we don't want to see any closer; and that's the one place we're trying to get to! And that's just where we can't get, nohow. We've come the wrong way altogether, seemingly. We can't get down; and if we did get down, we'd find all that green land a nasty bog, I'll warrant. Phew! Can you smell it?' He sniffed at the wind.

'Yes, I can smell it,' said Frodo, but he did not move, and his eyes remained fixed, staring out towards the dark line and the flickering

Just as I have suggested having pre-writing rituals, I recommend creating a clear end-of-the-day ritual to help you decompress. It's about saluting the fact that you have achieved another brick, or row of bricks, in the wall.

As I described in *The Reason to Write*, I tend to set myself specific daily wordage goals. I do this because it works for me. It may not work for you. But I suggest trying it, as it's satisfying and simple.

Before starting a new book, I write the title of the book at the top of an A4 sheet, and then list numbers all the way down the left-hand margin of the page, like this:

<u>The Reason to Write</u>

1.
2.
3.
4.
5.
6.
7.
etc. etc.

At the end of my writing day, I write the daily wordage and the cumulative amount beside the number.

The other thing I do, which is incredibly important, is to back the day's writing up. Again, this is something that can be done in a hundred ways. I personally simply add the manuscript file to an email and send it to myself.

As someone who has lost a lot of work over the years, I can vouch for spending a few seconds to make sure it's not just on your computer.

NOTES

The Time Machine

An Invention

By
H. G. Wells

London
William Heinemann
MDCCCXCV

The following notes were published in *The Reason to Write* and are reproduced here because they may be useful to solve specific problems, answer specific questions, and illustrate the nuts and bolts of the writer's life and craft.

Please Remember: The only way to grasp anything in a meaningful way is through an organic process of zigzag experience, rather than studying it A to Z.

As with any creative art, perfecting by doing is the essence of writing.

Over the following pages I will showcase a variety of random points which, when grouped as a collection, constitute the essence of the writing craft. It's important there's no order, but that they're taken all together – like individual fragments of mosaic forming a greater whole.

Beginnings

The start of a book is very important to me, but then again it's not very important at all. The way I work is to lay a foundation stone at the beginning of the first page. The stone is a line which blows me away with what I consider to be a gleaming gemstone of letters and words.

As I work on the first chapter, I keep looking back to the initial line, reading it over and over. By enthusing myself with how dazzling it is, I bathe in the warm blush of glory at my self-praise. More often than not, the first line gets changed as the book develops. I'll either end up starting the story somewhere else, or axe the first pages and cut to the chase.

But that doesn't matter.

What matters is that the first lines and paragraphs get you into the right mindset – giving you confidence so you're up to the challenge of writing the entire book.

Samples

One of my friends in Morocco is a master carpenter named Mr. Reda.

What I like about him most is that when he says he can do something, he does it. There's no boasting or tittle-tattle, but rather a body of work which speaks for itself. I once asked him the secret of his success. He replied:

'When I'm not sure how to complete the job at hand, I make samples. They demonstrate various kinds of carpentry that will be needed. The important thing is they are not executed to demonstrate anything to the client. I don't show them to anyone. Rather, they are done to demonstrate to me I have the skill to undertake the job.'

I always think of Reda's words when I have to write something daunting. And, following his example, I open a fresh page on my computer, or turn to a blank page in my journal, and scribble down samples – proof to myself that I'm worthy of the task at hand.

Fights

I recently had to write a fight scene for a novel and found myself stressing over it for days on end. I was anxious because fights tend to be a wild rumpus of action, emotion, and commotion, in which all kinds of actions and emotions occur.

In the frenzy it's easy to lose yourself, and the characters, without leading to any clear point of resolution. At times of stress, when I don't know how to handle the thing I have to write, I leave the work desk and go sit in a sagging yellow armchair in the corner of my study. My 'thinking chair', it always helps me come up with a solution in an almost magical way.

Time and again I would get up, go sit in the thinking chair, and turn the fight scene I had conceived over in my head. But each time I did so, the more stressed I became. Then, on the morning I had planned to write the scene, the thinking chair gave me what I needed – the greatest stage fight ever written, from *The Princess Bride*. Anyone who remembers the cliff-top scene will recall how the masked protagonist Westley battles with Inigo Montoya. It's a scene I know incredibly well because I've drooled over it so often – both on the screen and while reading the screenplay. Playing it back to myself in the thinking chair, I broke it down step by step.

Then, I laid the action over my own proposed fight scene. Through some kind of creative osmosis I found the template carried over and gave me what I needed to write a fight of my own.

Dialogue

Writers get worked up about dialogue far more than they should.

When I started writing books, Doris Lessing ordered me to take a tape recorder, get onto the top deck of a London bus, and to record the people behind me. 'Go and listen to what you've recorded,' she said. 'And, if it doesn't help, transcribe the tape.' I did as she suggested, and found myself appreciating that dialogue is the most normal kind of writing of all.

What's important is not to suffocate conversation in masses of direction – who said what and how. The authors whose work I respect most highly – people like Bruce Chatwin and Mark Salzman – handle dialogue as a series of fine-tuned movements in a dance. The lines are elegant, fast, and sensitive, with the writer taking a back seat, allowing the characters to shine.

Look through any of my books and you'll see I use a very standard technique for dialogue. From time to time I try and elaborate, embarrassed it's so simple. But I almost always rework it to the tried-and-tested template which has served me so well for so long.

Description

Different writers handle description in different ways.

A great many authors go heavy on it, to the point they're writing poetry in prose form. Preferring to tell the story as simply as possible, I throw in pinches of description along the way, and rarely write description for the sake of description. I dislike pages and pages of gloopy, treacle-like description that bogs the reader down.

The way I regard it, if you're cooking with good quality ingredients there's no need to smother them in sauces. Present them with simplicity and they'll be all the more delicious to those eating the meal.

When describing a character and their arc through a book, I like to build on the layers of observational description as I go. Along with everything else related to writing, the important thing is to keep writing. If you find the text is coming out laden with descriptive prose, then keep going.

Don't stress.

You can always trim it down or tweak it later.

Historical

I'm a believer that all writers should experiment, just as I believe writers who churn out the same novel again and again because they know it'll sell are duping themselves and their readers.

Those are two of the reasons why I tried my hand at historical fiction and wrote *Timbuctoo*. Set in 1816, the book tells the true-life story of the first white Christian to visit the African El Dorado and live to tell the tale. Having not written historical fiction before, I agonized over the process far too much, rather than just getting down to it and trying my luck.

As I've already described, I started by writing the story as a screenplay, before jumping through dozens of self-imposed hoops to prepare me for the task. The point I want to make here is that by writing historical fiction you have the chance to time travel in a way few other creative people ever have the opportunity to do.

Like most authors, I slip into the books I am writing, and I dwell there in a hollow deep under the ground. When I think back to the books I've written, *Timbuctoo* was the most intense experience of all because it dragged me through the Sahara as a slave, and into the high-life and low-life worlds of Regency London. Lifting the blinkers on the furthest limits of my creativity, it taught me far more than I'd ever have hoped for when I began.

Inspiration

My advice to anyone who's listening is to allow yourself to be inspired in every imaginable way. I've written about how mentors have helped me on the writing journey, by helping me to think in new ways. Multiple mentors are so incredibly useful, because they all think and act differently.

One example is the traveller and novelist Bruce Chatwin, to whom I owe a great debt. Chatwin was critically important not least because he was utterly original. My favourite book of his is the travelogue *The Songlines*.

Somewhere near the middle of that book is a big section of random material in italics. A collection of miscellaneous notes from his journeys, it's labelled simply, 'From the Notebooks'. I adore it because it stirs the reader up and sets them free – free to imagine, to wonder, and to dream.

Humour

A long time ago I overhead a young man asking his sister how to pick up a girl. The advice offered was this:

'Make her laugh, because if she laughs she'll give you her time, and if you get her time you'll win her heart.'

That sentence has been swimming round my head for decades – not because I ever used it to pick up girls, but rather because I used it to write. From my early days as a would-be author I felt guilt that anyone out there should be expected to read my work, and that by giving it to them I was forcing myself on them.

So, by tapping into the advice I'd caught on the wind, I devised a way of making myself feel better by making others laugh. Without quite realizing how I was doing it, I wove humour into my writing – laying it on thick. As a result I found I could set up ideas and thinking which would have been laborious to do without the magic of humour.

The very finest form of humour I've come across is the kind edged with poignancy, so the reader is left feeling moved. When done perfectly, the effect is so subtle you almost don't realize it's taken place at all.

Harnessing

When I hear writers moaning on and on about how they don't know what to write, I find myself yelling:

'Make a list of random people you've known and places you've been to!'

Stare at the names, pick out four people and four places, then let your imagination take over.

So that I don't come across as a complete phoney, I just tried it myself.

Here are my random people and places:

- Mr Gooderson, my prep-school science teacher who wore a wig and was obsessed with Ordinance Survey maps.
- James Labouchere, the prefect at my boarding school who built an aeroplane in metalwork which nosedived during a rugby match.
- Sir Wilfred Thesiger, my great friend and hero, who crossed the Empty Quarter of Arabia twice on foot.
- Helena Edwards, my father's secretary, known by the mystic George Gurdjieff as 'Blonde No. 24'.
- The Royal Bombay Yacht Club, a favourite haunt, where I lived when it was at its most rat-infested and run down.
- The village of Narok, in Kenya's Rift Valley, where I stayed as a student in the mid-eighties.
- Gangtok, capital of Sikkim, in northern India.
- A laundromat in Alice Springs where I once had one of the most interesting conversations of my life.

With the random list at hand, I scribble the names in circles on a fresh sheet of paper, like little islands, and start conjuring a story.

Don't overthink this exercise.

When people start off writing they're constantly overthinking when instead they should be allowing their imagination to run free.

So, doing it super-fast, I see the story set in the thirties of a trailblazing woman with flaxen yellow hair. Irrepressible and adventurous, she crisscrosses the world in search of a secret – a secret which will make sense of a map left to her by an elderly explorer in Sikkim.

Little by little, the layers of the story emerge.

I don't wrestle with the imagination, but rather let the story emerge from the darkness, like air bubbles percolating up through water. Force it, and the well of inspiration will run dry. If nothing comes to mind then go off and run errands, answer emails, or prune the roses. Whether you like it or not the story will keep flashing into your head as your mind works away.

Lists

Much of what I do as a writer is geared so that I don't cool down.

Sometimes I get to my desk and just can't face writing the next chapter of the book I'm working on. So what I do is to do something else – something complementary. My holy grail is to do work I'm in the mood for. And if I'm not in the mood for writing a heavy chapter, I do something more spontaneous and fun.

And, on days when I'm barely functioning at all, I make lists.

Lists of characters for novels I will write.

Lists of places I'd like to visit.

Lists of oddities.

Lists of interesting facts gleaned from Wikipedia.

And even lists of lists.

When I'm a little more engaged, I put meat on the bones of the lists. I'll let you into a secret to show you what I mean. A week ago, I couldn't face writing a chapter for this book, so I made a list of dozens of points which concern me as a writer – everything from humour to writing lists.

The list sat on my desktop until this afternoon.

Opening it up, I started writing entries for the various listings, and that's how this section came into being.

Brown Water
I've written elsewhere about getting started, but want to say once again that you have to dive in, have faith in yourself, and keep going. It's very easy to stress over the quality of the first pages. More likely than not they'll be uneven, jumbled, and confused. Of course they will be, and there's absolutely nothing wrong with that. Almost every book I've written has a different beginning to the one appearing in the first draft. The first thirty pages of a double-spaced manuscript tend to be the rusty brown water issuing forth from a tap which has been turned off tight. Open the tap wide, let the water flow, and come back to the start when you've crossed the finish line.

First Sentences
There's little so sacred to me as first sentences.

Even though they may ultimately be tweaked or rewritten, I usually know when I've got them right. Where possible I try to keep them short and sharp, and to ensure they lead on to a bigger point. An exception is the opening of my historical novel, *Timbuctoo*. Following the style of the novels of the time I allowed it the time and space it deserved.

Here's a list of first sentences which made the final cut in a selection of my books:

Godman: The Blackpool Grand had hosted the crème de la crème of entertainment in its time, from vaudeville to full musical extravaganzas, and even pantomime.

Travels With Nasrudin: On the eve of my sixth birthday, my father tucked me into bed. 'Are you excited for tomorrow?' he asked.

Jinn Hunter: Book One – The Prism: The vaults beneath the Bank of England, on London's Threadneedle Street, were utterly silent, as they were on any other night.

Jinn Hunter: Book Two – The Jinnslayer: As Oliver passed the executioner's hood back to Amalorous, he found himself sitting on a pile of sour old straw in Morrock's room again.

Hannibal Fogg and the Supreme Secret of Man: From the snow-laden crags of the Hindu Kush, the vast army of Alexander, King of the Macedonians and subjugator of the known world, seemed to move in total silence.

Paris Syndrome: On the morning of her fifth birthday, Miki Suzuki sat perched on her grandfather's knee, at the edge of the porch in the family home, a short distance from Sendai.

Casablanca Blues: The windowless walls at Acme Telesales were painted slate grey.

Scorpion Soup: When I was young and foolish, but so certain I was wise, I took any work offered.

Eye Spy: The waiting room of Dr. Amadeus Kaine's practice was panelled in antique mahogany and smelled of Indian lemongrass.

Timbuctoo: A pair of ornate Queen Anne braziers were crackling at either end of the opulent meeting room, warming the extremities, and leaving the fifty gentlemen seated at the central mahogany table wishing they had worn their woollen underwear instead.

In Arabian Nights: The torture room was ready for use.

The Caliph's House: There was a sadness in the stillness of dusk.

House of the Tiger King: The men had lost their smiles and their cheap grins.

In Search of King Solomon's Mines: An inky hand-drawn map hung on the back wall of Ali Baba's Tourist Emporium.

Trail of Feathers: The trail began at an auction of shrunken heads.

Sorcerer's Apprentice: We failed to realize it was an omen when it came.

Beyond the Devil's Teeth: A maze of passageways stretched in all directions.

Belief
'The Emperor's New Clothes' is a story that has seeped down deep into the marrow of my bones. The older I get, the more I find myself seeing shadows of the story all around me – it's everywhere.

Our society seems to be constructed on the flawed foundations on which the much-loved tale took place. Just as the emperor was naked, a great many of the people society champions as heroes are vacuous and (in my opinion) third-rate. But no one seems to burst the bubble like the little boy in the crowd did. I used to get very worked up indeed about how droves of untalented people make it to stardom. When I was discussing this with my father one afternoon in the days before his death, he said:

'Forget about all those time-wasters. They live fleeting lives with fleeting impact. Instead, strive to be original – to be someone whose work is on a grand scale and is different. Believe in yourself. Not in a half-hearted way, but with absolute conviction.

Never doubt your ability – not for a moment – and there'll be nothing in which you cannot succeed.'

Word Counts

Perhaps it's because I'm rather obsessive by nature, or because I like working towards a goal, I've always found noting down a daily word count to be the sure-fire method of staying on track.

My father used to write between seven and ten thousand words a day, and that was on a manual typewriter. I described how it sounded at the start. It was like interminable machine-gun fire. It's because of him I force myself to write an unreal daily wordage – because what I'd heard throughout my childhood was my 'normal'.

Only now do I realize there was nothing normal about it at all.

I've just had a quick look online and found the daily output of a range of authors. In some cases they're remarkably low. The point is not how much you write, but rather that you write. Do the same small amount each day and it adds up.

According to a range of Internet sites here's a tally of daily wordage:

Author	Words
Tom Wolfe	135
Ernest Hemingway	500
Graham Greene	500
Philip Pullman	1100
Mark Twain	1500
Charles Dickens	2000
Anthony Trollope	3000
Enid Blyton	6000
Michael Crichton	10,000

When planning a book, I give myself a strict writing schedule to keep to, and do my best to stay on course. I've written about this in the main text, so you'll find more elsewhere. The output I manage depends on the amount of creativity required. On a non-fiction book I strive towards 5000 words a day. On a regular fiction book I should be able to get down 3500 or 4000. And on a fantasy work – like the volumes in my *Jinn Hunter* series – I'll be pleased with 3000 to 3500.

I'm not pretending for a moment writing 5000 words a day isn't a challenge. Of course it is. But, do it every day for a week, then a month, and another, and your strength builds, as your narrative voice is itself fortified.

Noting down wordage is the one reliable method I know of moving forward.

But don't overdo it.

As with exercising, it's far too easy to do too much on day one – or in week one – and then get burned out. Burnout is the last thing a writer wants. It can set you back months or even years.

Worst of all, it can make a writer hate the craft.

Backups

We've all lost precious work, and I've probably lost more than anyone I know.

The reason can be chalked down to general carelessness. My advice is to do a daily backup in several ways.

When I have finished for the day, I rename the file I'm using with the day's date or the total wordage. Either is fine. Then, I store the draft on my computer's desktop, on an external hard drive, and (most importantly) I email it to myself.

As with almost everything connected to writing, the secret is to have a routine which is followed without thinking. Don't worry if the work you're backing up isn't edited – what matters is that it's safe and secure.

Momentum
Book writing is founded on momentum.

You don't have to be a super-genius to write books, but you have to keep the pressure up. In my thinking it's like the steam engine heading south to north. There'll be uphill stretches and downhill ones too, frequent and infrequent stops, fair conditions and driving rain.

To write the book you have to pace yourself, and ensure that whatever the conditions thrown at you, you keep going towards the distant horizon. Far too many writers like to drone on about the magical process of writing books. They're numbskulls, because there's relatively little magic needed.

But there is hard work.

Do the work by staying in the groove and the book writes itself. And the tried and tested way to stay in the groove is to maintain the head of steam, page after page, steam that'll get you to the very last line.

Introductions
When I wrote my first travel book – entitled *In Gondwanaland* (subsequently renamed *Beyond the Devil's Teeth*), I put an introduction at the front. It went on and on about my motives to write the book, and what I'd hoped to achieve.

Unable to get it published, I used to carry the manuscript around in a plastic bag and show it to anyone who'd take a look. One evening I was invited to a dinner party at which numerous members of the literati were already installed. An established writer present said he'd heard from the host about my book. As if by magic I pulled it out from under my chair. He took a look, flicking through the lengthy introduction.

'As writers we're in the gemstone business,' he said. 'And chopping out work which gets in the way is like faceting a gem. No one reads introductions in any case. Either call it Chapter One, or delete it – which is what I'd suggest you do.'

And that's exactly what I did.

Appendices
I'm an admirer of appendices because they allow a writer to present work which supports the main text, but which doesn't slow the reader down. Publishers loathe appendices because they often go unread, and because they take extra paper – paper which costs money.

My book *Trail of Feathers* has two appendices – one on flora-based hallucinogens of the Upper Amazon, and another dealing with the Shuar tribe of former head-shrinkers. I had to fight tooth and nail to get the appendices included, and only succeeded because I had started off by demanding the right to produce five of them.

Glossaries

As with appendices, glossaries are fodder for an editor's red pen.

Publishers dislike long explanations, and tend to insist they're never read, cost paper, and are time-consuming and therefore expensive to proofread.

My own thinking is to include a glossary if you can stand to write it, because it provides balance to the meal. In my *Jinn Hunter* series, the glossaries run to twenty thousand words and are a central pillar of the story.

Collecting Words

Writers love words. It's as simple as that.

We may not admit it in public, but to us they're delicious, like hand-cut mosaics set lovingly into a decorative frieze. I try to use words that are in regular use, so the reader doesn't have to reach for a dictionary (not that anyone ever bothers to these days). At the same time, I do my best to use a variety of vocabulary so that I don't subject the reader to undue tedium.

In my wider life I collect words that are especially delectable, either for their sound, their meaning, or both. Words, for instance like 'petrichor' – the bewitching smell of first rain. Or 'pettifogging', being unnecessarily trivial, or 'coddiwomple' – to travel in a purposeful manner towards a distant destination. Most of the words I note down are found in newspapers, books, and spoken on the radio. I heard one this morning and scribbled in into my journal right away – sulphurous. I've heard it before, of course, but have never used it. Can't wait to slip it into something soon.

Kubrick

I've been a life-long fan of the celebrated film director Stanley Kubrick – not because all his work is amazing, but because he stretched himself and experimented.

Far too many directors go on and on making the same kind of movie, just as too many authors keep on writing the same kind of book. My belief is that to grow you have to stretch yourself, in the way Kubrick did. Look at the movies he made, and you quickly see they span a wide variety of genres. More interested in his own learning curve as a director, he gave little time to making movies the studios, or even the film-going public, wanted.

Kubrick's movies span the following genres:
- Horror – *The Shining*
- Science Fiction – *2001: A Space Odyssey*
- War – *Full Metal Jacket*
- Comedy – *Dr. Strangelove*
- Crime – *A Clockwork Orange*
- Mystery – *Eyes Wide Shut*
- Romance – *Lolita*
- Action – *Spartacus*
- Drama – *Fear and Desire*

Taking Notes

Not all writers take notes, but most do. Of those, a great many probably do so to appear erudite or worthy. Pulling out their Moleskine notebooks at a dinner party, twanging back the elasticated band, they strain to seem self-important, or at least interesting.

In my opinion, the only reason to take notes is to register something which could be fitted in at a later date. I'd never share my notes, as they are private and wouldn't make sense to anyone else.

More often than not I scribble down details – such as the cost of something, like a ferry journey across the bay in Cochin, or the waxy complexion of a croupier at a roulette table in Colombo.

As a child, my parents encouraged me to take concise notes on everything new I experienced. The task became a cornerstone of my enthusiasm for collecting people. Alas, my most precious notebook from that time was confiscated by a brutish monocle-wearing master at my prep school.

I find listing details in bullet points to be an efficient method to get the key facts down. For instance, a note taken last night at a dinner that was loathed by absolutely everyone invited:

- Sixteen random people, all sombre, most self-centred.
- Boy, girl, boy, girl down the table festooned with lemon-scented flowers.
- Man to my right dandruff like first winter snow.
- Glass eye. Scarred right hand. Slight lisp.
- Woman across table trepanned herself in about '66 with a man called Mellen.
- Claimed to have known my grandfather and Timothy Leary in Tangier.
- Meal featured quails and undercooked turnips served whole. Gravy curious shade of powder blue.
- Everyone forced to give a three-minute speech. Talked about shrunken head techniques of the Shuar. Went down like a lead balloon.
- Madame G. promised to show me her box of bull bezoars if I visit again next week.

Anthologies

In the last year I have produced sixteen full anthologies of my work, arranged by theme, an idea which came about as a procrastination.

At first I planned to publish a single anthology. But, the more I considered it, the more it seemed right to do a series, and in a way no publisher would ever allow. As with anything I do, it's done because it's of interest to me, and me alone.

Taking selections from my existing corpus of work, and adding to them dozens of new pieces, was an intensely interesting exercise. I recommend that all writers create anthologies. As with anything else, it's easier not to bother, but hugely worthwhile when complete. Most importantly though, the exercise gives one an opportunity to regard one's work in a new way.

Wikipedia Vortex

The internet has provided even the most challenged writer with a stream of detail, information, and phantasmagorical delight, to use in any way they wish. When I was new to writing books, I used to amass hundreds of pages of neatly typed notes that I'd first made by hand. I did this because I was so fearful that the task of writing the book would confound me.

As the years have gone by, and as I have got increasingly confident, I've done less and less research in advance. Instead, I've mined material online and from books as and when it's needed. If it's being done online – especially on Wikipedia – you have to take care.

Don't get me wrong, I'm Wikipedia's No. 1 fan.

But it's far too easy to be sucked into the Wikipedia Vortex. You start by looking up the currency of Gambia (resist the urge, it's *dalasi*) and, next thing you know, you've slalomed your way through a hundred articles on everything from bluebottles to Blackbeard, and half the writing day has gone.

Editing
As with proofreading, it's essential to get your work edited if you're releasing it yourself. Most professional writers agree that in recent years publishers have shirked on having editorial work done. As with everything else, it's chalked down to cost-cutting. This means books with terrible plot holes get launched, like ships with great gashes down the side. The best-case scenario is to find an editor who you like, and to work with them book by book. They will get to know how you write, and what your strengths and failings are. Most importantly, they'll know to be sensitive with their criticisms, and to polish your work rather than reshaping it.

Correcting
This is important:

If you follow my example and publish work yourself, you MUST be certain there are no typos or obvious mistakes. I can't stress this strongly enough. Typos and errors of any kind will leave you open to attack – whether you care about condemnations or not. So, it's critically important to have work proofed numerous times.

I tend to get a manuscript proofed by four different people before typesetting, and then again by another four afterwards. Even then, a typeset book should be read by as many friends, fans, and family as you can muster. You have to explain to them though what they are being asked to proof for. Even though I try to brief friends what I want and don't want, one or two always give lists of punctuation they regard as inappropriate.

Another key point is that everyone picks up different stuff. There's a professional proofreader I tend to use who is completely challenged at the job. He misses almost everything – even the most glaring errors staring him in the face. But every time I give him a manuscript, he'll find two or three mistakes everyone else has missed.

For that reason his work is worth its weight in gold.

Daily Read
I am a fast writer but a slow reader – notched down to my dyslexia. I abhor reading through work I have written line by line, making sure the grammar's right. I do it nonetheless, and find reading through my day's output before leaving my desk at the end of the day is very useful indeed.

In the same way, reading through and correcting the previous day's pages saves a writer like me hundreds of hours of editing work later. Of course you will have to go through newly written work plenty of times before it's published, but early read-throughs tend to pick up on errors which might later be missed.

Listening
This is especially for all the dyslexics out there:

As I'm such a slow reader, I find the best way to stay focused is to get my computer to read passages of text back to me. My Apple Mac is set up so that if I highlight the text, then press Apple+X, a voice reads aloud. This is especially useful when I am editing work – because I can quickly make small changes as the voice continues reading. I find hearing text allows me to pick up errors I wouldn't otherwise notice – like a missing article or pronoun.

eBooks
Publishers like to try to impress upon authors how, by some far-fetched alchemy, they'll get their work released in eBook form. It's nuts of course, because nothing is simpler than getting your book encoded as an eBook. Most of the time it costs very little indeed. My advice to any author is to retain eBook rights when knocking out the terms of a contract, and get an independent eBook firm to put out your work directly. That way you get to keep all the revenue and, even more important, overall control.

Americanization
There are plenty of firms online which will change the spelling and formatting of your manuscript so you can release it in the United States, or vice versa. From my experience, if you are releasing your book directly, it's well worth having a British and an American edition, with separate ISBN numbers and barcodes. The transfers are not expensive, and they open up an entirely new market. Of course, Americans will read British versions, and Brits will read US editions, but they tend to prefer their own.

Motivation
Procrastination, boredom, despondency, and general self-doubt have surely been the curse of writers since books were written on clay tablets – no surprise in that. After all, we're taking a blank tablet, blackboard, scroll, sheet of paper, computer screen, and are adorning it with a stream of letters and words, pulled from the ether. All writers tend to hone methods of mitigating doubt, and motivating themselves.

What works for me is to read random passages from The Shelf of Wretched Reads. It's proof in an instant that your work is way better than some of the most celebrated names in the business.

Chair
If you're serious about becoming a writer, go out and invest in the best, most expensive chair you can afford. You'll be sitting there for hundreds of hours, so get one with excellent lumbar support, which doesn't creak and grind when you move.

A friend who spends her life straightening out bad backs once gave me a top tip – search on eBay for a refurbished company chair. She said the ones from meeting rooms tend to be the least worn, and that there are lots still available from high-end firms which went bankrupt after the financial crash, as well as in the dark days of Covid-19.

Confidence

I've touched on confidence elsewhere, and quite rightly so.

Fear of failure is something uniting almost all creative people, and is one of the greatest threats we face. Meanwhile, confidence is a Promised Land you only reach by sailing out towards the horizon, rather than going round and round in circles.

Write twenty books and you can't help but acquire a hefty dose of confidence. But beware: stop writing for a prolonged period and the confidence dissipates as though it were never there at all.

When You Know

At the time we were expecting our daughter, Ariane, my wife asked the midwife how to know when she was in labour. The answer given was this:

'If you're wondering whether or not you're in labour, you're not in labour.'

The same goes for being a real writer.

If you're not sure whether you are one, then you're not.

Being a real writer is a condition, a state of mania and melancholy, a psycho zone controlling every aspect of your day. It's to be gloriously on the edge, in a place most people hardly even realize exists.

Open Sesame!

Follow your heart, write books, and doors will open that were previously locked, or even invisible.

This is something I witnessed first-hand with my father. Clattering away in his study day after day, he released a stream of original work over decades. With each new book that appeared, more opportunities arrived. Many of them were the kind non-creative people rarely encounter.

I've described the mixture of characters populating my childhood, a time when my father was at his creative height. They had all been lured to Langton House as a result of my father's books. Many were celebrated writers, scientists, and thinkers, but many others were unknown. Those were the ones I found most interesting because they'd lived full-spectrum lives.

In addition to the regulars, new visitors arrived all the time – visitors bearing opportunities.

On one occasion a pair of gold-plated Rolls-Royces slunk up the drive, bearing an entourage from an oil-rich state in the Far East. Having followed my father's work since his youth, the Head of State wanted him to redesign the nation's educational system.

As an author, my life also led to opportunities and encounters I'd have never thought possible. They appear when you least expect them, and are a direct result of churning out material and releasing it into the wild.

My books have taken me to experiences I never expected – from visiting Emperor Haile Selassie's treasure vaults beneath the presidential palace in Addis Ababa, to one-on-one meetings with the Dalai Lama and Mother Teresa, to high-level meetings at top secret diplomatic missions, Boeing Aviation, and the United Nations.

Obelix Syndrome
Do you remember how, in the *Asterix* books, happy-go-lucky Obelix had fallen into the cauldron of magic potion as a baby? While the other Gauls in the village needed a regular top-up of the potion, he didn't, because he'd consumed so much that he was primed with strength for life.

My take on writing is inspired by Obelix.

If you write masses – and I mean MASSES – then an extraordinary thing happens, an alchemy. It's what Doris told me was 'getting to the higher ground'. Read any of her books – especially the later ones – and you feel Obelix in the fluidity and the strength of her narrative voice. The voice was so fluent, so gloriously warmed up, that there was nothing she couldn't write, reason, discuss, or explain.

As I have said, I am no great linguist, and have always struggled with languages. On the rare occasions I have been steeped in a language, I've managed to run free for minutes, hours, or even days. The sensation is like cycling without training wheels for the first time – as it was for me when Greville taught me to cycle.

Writing fluency is very similar to linguistic fluency.

In order to be absolutely fluent you have to write colossal amounts of text. I'm not talking about a few chapters every so often – or a book every couple of years. I'm talking about four, five, or six books a year. Get in that zone, and stay there – like a speed cyclist streamlined in the peloton – and you'll reach a plateau few writers have ever known.

Please don't tell me with all the tools at our disposal that it's such a huge feat of trial and tribulation to knock out a good-sized chunk of pages in a day. Of course it's not. For the Victorians, the prevailing convention was very much one of industry, whereas in our time it's quite the opposite. Writers, and would-be writers, drone on and on about the craft of writing, while doing relatively little of it. It's something that's plain wrong and needs correcting.

Literary Identity
With the conventional publishing model – the one I've railed against throughout this book – there's almost no way an author can ever reach Doris Lessing's 'higher ground'. Unless you're a fantasy novelist churning out blockbusters hand over fist, publishers will want a book only every year or two. It's the publishers who created the myth that writers can't produce more than they do. In a way, the myth reminds me of the great misguided belief in sport – how running a four-minute mile was impossible… before it was run by Roger Bannister.

There's no question most writers are capable of writing a lot more. The problem is that the publishing houses are incapable of selling more. And, as I've said over and over, all they care about is making cold hard cash, so they'll never release a book that's not expected to sell in droves.

A great many of my friends are authors. As you'd imagine we are supportive of each other's work, having watched our various careers and projects trundling along.

Until the new model of direct publishing came along, the only way around the clampdown was to create more than one literary identity, whether the publishers realized it or not. My grandfather, who was running like a finely tuned engine throughout the twenties and thirties, knocked out up to half a dozen books a year. It was the only way he could survive from his pen.

Raising a small family, and living on his written work, he had no choice but to write under an ever-increasing stable of pseudonyms. His pen names included: John Grant, Richard Drobutt, Raoul Simac, Rustam Khan-Urf, Syed Iqbal, Sheikh Ahmed Abdullah, Bahloal Dana, Ibn Amjed, and even 'Afghan'.

Doing What Works
Most of what I have to say about writing is based on straightforward thinking, and there's nothing more straightforward than doing what works for you. Although I've described my own personal writing methods, I celebrate those of others who have developed a method and run with it.

A perfect example is the Sicilian novelist Andrea Camilleri, who died in 2019, aged ninety-three. Other than being a talented author of detective fiction, the extraordinary thing about Camilleri was the way he worked on a template. Rarely deviating from it, he produced thirty novels – eight a year – each one with eighteen chapters, and a hundred and eighty pages.

Camilleri is proof, if anyone needs it, that you can come to writing late (he was in his mid-sixties when he became a bestseller), producing a full body of work.

In Character
Thirty years ago, Daniel Day-Lewis won a Best Actor Oscar for his portrayal of Christy Brown, the Irish writer and painter who could only move his left foot. Unable to sleep one night, I caught a documentary about the making of the movie *My Left Foot*.

The image that stuck with me was Daniel Day-Lewis on a break between scenes. While all the other cast and crew were happily tucking into their lunch, Day-Lewis was slouched in his chair, limbs seized up as though he actually suffered the cerebral palsy he was portraying so skilfully.

The point I want to make is that, especially when slipping into the world of fiction, it's helped me to remain in character throughout the day. I'm not pretending I become all the characters I write about, but elements of each one root themselves within me. As such, staying in character as I break from the desk enables me to stay in the zone.

Collaborations
I am enthusiastic about collaborating with other creative people – whether it's for an anthology, or a book which observes a particular subject from different angles. In the same way friends exercise together at the gym, having a buddy can make the process of writing far less isolating.

Collaborations are a way of pooling common ideas, building on shared interests, and stretching oneself in directions that may well have been unthinkable before.

For both new and established authors, it can be a way of expanding one's readership. Many writers have an overlap in their audience, but very few share exactly the same set of readers.

The only problem with collaborations is they tend to hit the buffers unless there's one key person charged with keeping the project on track. On occasions when I have been approached about a potential collaboration, I've pitched in only when there's a charitable angle. Part of the reason for this is that the division of royalties between numerous authors is like untangling a bowl of spaghetti.

On-going Tweaks
This is a small point but an important one.

When writing books it's good practice to leave as little work for later as you can. Getting a book in shape to be published is a hard slog, and so if you can reduce the number of misspellings and basic corrections, and other simple stuff, you'll save yourself days, possibly weeks of hard grind.

In my experience it's much easier to clean text fast when you're in the moment. Later you'd have to remember the precise sense of a passage. Before ending a day's stint in the chair, try to correct spellings and grammar, and basic facts.

Again, beware you don't find yourself slipping down the rabbit hole into the Wikipedia Wonderland of fact-checking – and for this reason I recommend checking at the end of the day, when you'll be only too keen to get away from your desk.

Originality
If there's one single thing I'd wish for a real writer to get from this book it's the importance of being original.

In many ways nothing else really matters to me.

I have always praised my children, Ariane and Timur, when they thought differently, as my sisters and I were rewarded by our own parents. Thinking different, and doing different, is profoundly important – especially as we live at a time in which everyone seems fixated on aping those around them.

Never be afraid to fall flat on your face from failure.

What matters is trying new things.

I say this knowing full well that both writing and reading fraternities can be mercilessly critical of anyone who experiments with fresh approaches. But, equally, they can be welcoming. After all, human history remembers trailblazers rather than those who simply regurgitate.

Payoffs
As a slow reader, I have always been drawn to books with plenty going on.

Aged about seven I'd lie in bed and read *The Guinness Book of Records* night after night, marvelling at so many wondrous feats all packed into a single book. Those world records were, in a way, payoffs. Read one and you were instantly amazed and satisfied, like a rat rewarded with a food pellet for getting through a maze.

In the same way *Guinness* provided payoffs, I have always done my best to provide them while writing books. It's far easier to succeed in this than you may think, and is achieved in considering material in a new way, turning it around on itself.

The best way to see what I mean and to learn the technique is to study Mark Salzman's *Iron and Silk*, itself a masterclass in payoffs. Through Salzman I learned to give the reader a payoff every page and a half.

Alternation

I'm not sure where I picked up a technique of alternating, but I am certain that I did – rather than invent it myself. By alternation, I mean having two, or even more, timelines or strands running through the book.

This was especially conspicuous in my novel *Hannibal Fogg and the Supreme Secret of Man*. In that book I used two clear timelines – almost a century apart. By alternating from one to the other I could keep the narrative moving along the tracks which satisfied me as the storyteller. I've used it in a lot of other books as well, as I find it allows me to sustain a kind of dynamism that might well be lost by writing in a more linear way.

Descriptive Detail

Writing books is like the growth and anatomy of a tree.

You need a good structure with firm roots, a thick trunk, and strong boughs to hold the maze of telescoping branches and twigs. But you need leaves as well – millions of them. Descriptive detail is like the foliage on a great, sprawling oak tree. Hold a single leaf in your hand and marvel at it in the same way you would do an individual fragment of description. Stripped of their leaves in winter, trees retain their form but are skeletal.

Out of all the elements of writing, I'd say writing fine description is more challenging than anything else. It's something with which to experiment and master, a skill which repays the time spent on it tenfold.

Peanuts

The last thing I'd ever do would be to tell real writers what to write or how to write it. All I can do is to explain what has worked for me and why. Over time, I have isolated a kind of formula which allows me to write simply and efficiently, while sucking in the material I need to include.

I mentioned Charles Schultz previously. He claimed to have reached a point at which he could make any point through his celebrated cartoon strip, *Peanuts*. In the same way, I like to think that over time I have learned to express even the most complex ideas through a simple matrix.

The challenge for a writer is to break the material down and to feed it to the reader in a way that's both entertaining and nourishing. For me this means a delicious smoothie of succinct sentences, paragraphs, and chapters. I could just as easily alter the mixture, packing it with unwieldy sentences, mind-numbing themes, and painful verbosity, but that would be to freeze the smoothie until it were a block of ice.

I'll leave it to you to decide which is easier for the reader to consume.

Brain Freeze

Sit at a desk for twelve hours and you feel as though your brain's been taken out of your head, frozen solid, whacked repeatedly with a baseball bat, and jammed back inside.

I have to admit I LOVE that feeling.

It's terrible I know, but it's proof I've created on a grand scale. I beg anyone reading this not to follow my example. Writing day after day to the point of brain freeze is tantamount to a suicide mission during a war.

It may get the job done, but it comes at a price.

Unfortunately for me, I'm pretty obsessive, so it means I attack anything which needs doing with a full-on barrage of raw enthusiasm.

After a few hours I get to a point at which I can't think about emails, paying bills, phoning friends, or even rooting about the fridge for something to eat.

At the end of a hard writing day I like to sit in a room lit with candles, and to turn my mind off so as to let it thaw. My kids always laugh at me when I'm in that state because I can't get through the complicated crime dramas they enjoy. Instead, I do what my father did when I myself was a child – I watch reruns of something I know inside out, like *Fawlty Towers*.

Sleep

When writing exceptionally long hours it's essential to get a solid night's sleep. Anything less than seven hours is likely to lead to second-rate work the next day.

In my experience there's absolutely no point in even trying to write anything if your brain is tired. That's because reworking second-rate text produced by a tired brain is far harder than coming up with first-rate passages later.

Throughout the day I monitor my levels of energy. If I get a sense my brain is fatigued, I stop everything and go and take a siesta. When grinding away at long novels I've found myself taking three or four fifteen-minute siestas in the same day. What works for me is to get into bed, power down, and get to the point at which I've just nodded off. If I can wake up a few minutes after that, I'm completely re-energized.

The other use of sleep – especially siestas – is to glimpse the next phase of my story play out in my mind's eye. I've used this technique in most of my novels, none more so than the *Jinn Hunter* books. I've found watching events take place on the stage of my mind works like nothing else.

Although I can never manage to remember entire dreams, I grab hold of individual details and fragments of storyline. Best of all, though, I love the way that when drifting into sleep, my mind makes associations. Remembering them as best I can, I weave them into the upcoming pages of my book.

Peaks, Troughs

There's absolutely no point in pushing writing output to the limit, so that what you're creating is coming out as mediocre. This sounds obvious but it's surprisingly easy to try and stay on the damned schedule at all costs. All of a sudden what you're turning out is shoddy because you're tired or drained of inspiration.

What I've found works is driving oneself very hard for a few days, then taking the foot off the production pedal just long enough to coast along for a while, before applying it hard again. As I've said elsewhere, when I start a book I'm relentless with production because it's far too easy to get side-tracked onto something else. You must get to the break-the-back stage before you can really allow yourself to coast – at least, that's what works for me.

The Ordinary

One afternoon I took a long, circuitous walk with a friend through the East End of London, back in the days when I lived there. I was ranting on about how I lived for oddity, and that normality bored me like nothing else. My friend turned to me and said:

'Never be afraid to embrace the ordinary.'

At the time I thought he was off his rocker. But, as the remark sank in and as I've progressed through my writing life, I realized how the comment was profound. The ordinary can be just as extraordinary as anything else. It's a matter of observing it though.

Turn the ordinary gently into the light, and allow it to shine.

In my earlier books I used to feature an ongoing rumpus of spectacular oddness and curiosity. But with time I've learned to slow down, and to observe what appears at first glance to be banal in new and mesmerizing ways.

Dyslexia

I drone on about dyslexia a great deal, probably because so few other writers do.

A stigma against dyslexics still prevails, although things are a whole lot better than when I was being punished at prep school for being so incompetent. I've released editions of my books in Open Dyslexic font (which is uneven, like text typed by a manual typewriter). And I myself use a whole range of homespun tricks to alleviate the effects of being so profoundly dyslexic.

These include getting my computer to read my text aloud, rather than struggling over reading it hour after hour. Another staple of mine is to set the background of the document I'm working on to grey, and to change the shade of it every day or so. I make bullet points in my notes, too, as they hone my focus, and of course I rely on spell correction like nothing else.

I encourage dyslexic writers to structure their work with mini ways to move forward and keep on track. But, most of all, I encourage them to take charge of their power of imagination.

In all likelihood it'll be second to none.

Spell Check

The spell correction on Microsoft Word, the program I write with, makes the life of dyslexic two-finger authors like me a whole lot better than it would be without it.

Even when I type fast, making loads of mistakes, they're underlined in red, or are simply corrected automatically. I have to admit though it drives me crazy when the spell correction doesn't recognize a word – or when it continually forces me to use American spelling (or British spelling if I'm using American variations). From time to time I play around with the settings, and get my computer to learn new words, but it invariably forgets them and resorts to what the Microsoft Mothership regards as right.

Grammar Check

While I favour spell check, grammar correction programs are my nemesis.

They're clearly not designed for anyone writing anything longer than a letter, and are certainly not intended for authors churning out books. I almost never have the grammar correction switched on, and if I do it's merely to laugh at the low quality of current programming.

No doubt over coming years AI will change the editing landscape entirely... even to the point of getting computers to write novels from scratch.

Perish the thought.

Dry Stone Wall
I was raised in a house where dictionaries were regarded as sacred books. My father would always encourage us children to look a word up if we didn't know its meaning. My love of words came from him, as well as my appreciation for keeping vocabulary simple and sentences succinct.

In my study there's a shelf of excellent dictionaries. I enjoy selecting a specific dictionary for a particular kind of word. I have a couple of pictorial dictionaries, too, in which the names of almost anything you could ever imagine are illustrated. They're especially useful when I need the precise word for a little-known stretch of rigging on a pirate ship, a blacksmith's tool, or something like that. I urge anyone who takes writing seriously to always look words up. It never ceases to surprise me how celebrated writers misuse words, and how their editors don't catch the mistakes.

I regard the text I'm writing as it were a dry-stone wall running along a road.

The words are pieces of stone which have to fit perfectly if the wall's going to exist as long as I'm hoping it will. I take great pleasure in selecting a perfectly shaped word for the space it will occupy, so that it will shine by itself and sit well with the other words around it.

Although I am an admirer of printed dictionaries, I recommend keeping a computer's default dictionary open when writing. The one on my Apple Mac is exceptionally good, and usually provides a line or two of precious etymology as well.

Work in Progress
As I have said elsewhere, I rarely, if ever, show work in progress to anyone. Likewise, I prefer not to read anyone else's half-finished writing. If you're a new writer it's best not to ever send anything to established authors unless you have asked permission. I'm sent masses of work – both completed and in progress – and always find myself wishing people would hold off until the work is pristine and as clean as it can be.

When I was a little boy at Langton House, Greville the storytelling carpenter was eventually replaced by a handyman named Stephen. As I remember it, his father was a bishop who'd questioned his own faith. Stephen was not a storyteller but a mathematician. I'm not sure how he came to be working at Langton House, but as a child I wasn't interested in the route he'd taken so much as the fact he was there.

Round about the time Stephen appeared, I'd been given a huge book of puzzles by my favourite aunt, Amina. I would lie on the lawn on my stomach, doing my best to solve the puzzles. The ones I liked most of all were the mazes – some of which were very intricate indeed. I remember working away at the puzzles one afternoon while Stephen was mowing the lawn. I'd do a few more twists and turns with my pencil, then rush over, get Stephen to turn the mower's engine off, and show him what I'd done.

The first five or six times I bothered him, he was polite. After that point, his patience strained, he cried through gritted teeth:

'Why don't you come back and show me when you've finished?!'
I thought for a moment, and replied with uncharacteristic honesty:
'Because you wouldn't tell me how well I'm doing nearly as much.'

That's how it is when a writer sends out half-finished work. They do it because they want to be patted on the head and told they're marvellous. This may make me sound stern – possibly sterner than I actually am – but I think it illustrates my thinking, thinking which is the essence of this entire book.

Real writers don't write for praise, they do so because they're writing for themselves.

Real Readers
Real authors love real readers, and there's nowhere I've found better readers than the Goodreads site.

As I've said, I regard the job of the writer as being to write for themselves, and that of the publisher as nonsensical in this day and age. Likewise, I think 'real' readers – the kind who follow one's work over years and champion it – have an important role to play.

They are our sounding boards.

And the more of a spectrum of them you can muster, the more useful the sounding board becomes. I've always found that everyone reads in their own way, and that women read quite differently to men. Indeed, much of the time women seem to read more accurately than men. Of all the many thousands of emails and letters I've received over the years, by far the most articulate ones have been from women. They've noticed details and asked questions about themes and sub-themes, whereas the majority of male readers writing to me have asked broad-spectrum questions... questions which seek to elevate them by association.

Publicity Quotes
As with anything else, breaking into the world of writing is partly (or rather largely) about credibility. That means even if your work is amazing, you have to persuade others it is, too. As a species we are communal, and strive to mitigate risk.

What better way to do that than to follow what other survivors are doing? When I started writing books I spent a lot of time networking in order to get publicity quotes from established authors. At one stage my life was dedicated full-time to getting quotes.

Each time I got a choice quote, I'd drop it into the stew served up in letter form to someone else, a little higher up the food chain. A great many of the people I wrote to with gushing letters never responded.

Surprisingly, a lot of them did.

I'm not going to come across well by admitting to this ruse, but please take my honesty into account:

When in the desperate-need-for-publicity-quotes racket, I used to write to elderly authors and wax lyrical about their first published book. Most established authors go on to publish work far more impressive than their initial offering. But in every writer's heart there's a soft spot for the firstborn.

Where possible you're best off striking up a correspondence, rather than asking for a quotation outright in the first message. If you want to get good quotes you have to work up to it – flattery first and requests second. The best plan of action is always to try and get a mixture of quotes, as I did with my first book *Beyond the Devil's Teeth*. I sent the manuscript to everyone I could think of – including the Pope, three ex-US Presidents, twelve Olympians, nine Nobel Laureates, and even a serial killer.

The way I saw it, languishing on death row, he had time on his hands.

Writing Routines
My writing method is all about routines.

I'm going to come across as a nutcase here, but I swore an oath of honesty to myself before starting this book, so here goes:

When I sit down to write a book I like to have a clean run ahead of me, like a well-prepared ski slope – a slope I've never skied before. As with a skier ready to set off, I've studied the map, and have planned a route. Despite the preparation, I'm aware there'll be unforeseen twists and turns, and patches where I have to jab my poles in and push really hard.

By nature I'm a creature of habit, and find nothing gets books written better or faster than routine. Some author friends inch forward little by little, taking months or even longer to complete a book. I prefer to rush headlong, so as to keep good continuity and, more importantly, to make sure that the book gets done.

Tricks of my trade include:
1. Have an outline on my desk, whether it's consulted or not.
2. Have a tally of what needs to be written on a particular day, and work towards it.
3. Reward myself for a hard day at the grind – even if it's only a takeout burrito with extra-hot sauce.

At the same time, I have certain objects on my desk when I'm writing. They change from book to book. Sometimes they'll be a little pile of red paperclips, or three blue gel pens – which I'll have neatly lined up and will never use.

But the key part of my routine happens at the end of the writing day.

If I've hit my writing target I add the number of words to the overall tally, and hopefully have reason to gloat. Then I straighten everything out for the following morning. Before leaving my workroom, I write the next day's goal on a sticky note and place it squarely beside the keyboard.

Whatever ritual you come up with, use it to get the best out of yourself.

In my opinion, rituals are of no service except to make the ski down the mountain easier and more pleasurable to achieve.

Procrastination
Procrastination is part of the creative process.

However terrible it may seem, it's critically useful – because it's the dream zone proving that we need inspiration in order to create. There's a danger in trying to eliminate procrastination, one that may well lead to far less original and inspired work. My advice is to allow oneself regular structured procrastination breaks. Safe zones, they're when you can turn your phone on, guzzle espresso, stare out the window, and allow your mind to slip away into a faraway realm.

The way I perceive it, daydreaming and procrastination are the waking forms of nocturnal dreaming. As such, they are the place at which the blurred mind creates wonder by zoning out of focus.

I've written about Wikipedia elsewhere, and will touch on it again here. As I usually research information as I move ahead, I generally resort to checking material online, or in reference books kept to hand. What works for me is to write on a scrap of paper exactly what I need to know before embarking on the online search. Diving aimlessly into the enchanted Wikipedia pool is accompanied by the danger of never emerging intact.

Giving in to procrastination, I give myself a challenge. Setting a timer and an alarm, I try and dredge up ten choice nuggets of information online within fifteen minutes.

Gaps
One of the most pleasing times while writing is when you're on a roll. All real writers know the feeling. To return to a skiing analogy again, it's like slaloming serenely down the mountain with the sun warming your face.

It's when you're a star, and everything's going oh-so-great.

But, ultimately, even the most skilled real writer hits a patch of ice.

You have to anticipate the rough ground and take immediate action – like a hospital emergency department with an action plan at the ready.

When in the middle of a book, I can usually ski around the patches of ice. This is because I'm worn in and ready for anything. But, especially in the early stages of a book, I get left high and dry like anyone else. The best thing to do is to leave three blank lines, and to come back to the trouble area later. The worst thing you can do is to drop everything and fall head-first into a hole.

The other time to leave a gap is when you need to slot in a small chunk of detail – like the name of a particular pistol your protagonist has just grabbed from an enemy soldier at dusk. In my case, the Wikipedia monster perched on my right shoulder is begging me to allow him two minutes to check out high-end German-made armaments, the kind used by special forces.

I never let the monster go anywhere near the internet.

We both know that two minutes will inevitably turn into an hour and a half of trawling the Wikipedia Wonderland.

Typing
Most of my close friends are writers and almost all of them are terrible typists.

Like me, the majority hammer out their books with two fingers.

My own excuse is that as a child I was given a pre-War Underwood Noiseless Typewriter to learn on. A great hulk of mechanical mastery, it sounded like a freight train clattering through the night towards the dawn. The noise wasn't the problem though, so much as the fact my young fingers couldn't apply sufficient pressure to get the keys to strike. So I ended up relying on my index fingers – as my father had done.

My grandfather, writer and savant The Sirdar Ikbal Ali Shah, who published seventy-four books, wrote them all by hand. My point is that it doesn't matter at all how you commit your work to paper. There'll always be a faster way to do it. But you are a creative writer, not a copy typist. So speed isn't important.

It's true I get worked up with myself from time to time at making so many mistakes. But I'm using a computer, unlike my father's generation, which was clattering away on manual and then electric typewriters. If anything, two-finger typing allows me to stare vacantly at the keyboard, and for my mind to wander as I'm doing so. Although I'm half-looking at the keys, I do so no more than I need to. My focus is tuned in to the creative frequency that's feeding me the upcoming lines of text.

Breaking the Back
Get past the halfway mark of a book and you're most likely to get to the end.

In the books I have written I've always found different stretches vary in their difficulty or ease. The first few chapters are usually the most onerous for me. Until I have the camber of the road worked out, I try too hard. But as I get into the swing of things, I find myself moving briskly forward. Get through the quicksand at the beginning, then up onto the wide plateau, and you'll probably be assured a good long run that'll take you to the other side of the halfway mark.

Get there in one piece and you will have broken the back of the book.

In my opinion this is the point to celebrate rather than when you write the last line. That's because the ending is a moment of sorrow, whereas the mid-point is proof you're on tip-top form.

Questioning
If there's one golden rule of book writing to nail up above your desk, it is:
NEVER QUESTION YOUR ABILITY!

They say if you want to dance like a pro you should practise as though no one is watching. The same is true for writing. If you want to take the craft to a whole new level, write as though no one will judge you. And remember to write for yourself.

Every time you question your ability, you smother the flame of creativity a little more. Remind yourself over and over that you're amazing. If you ever doubt it, read a random page grabbed from your Shelf of Wretched Reads.

Remember this: the more you write, and the more differing projects you work on, the stronger your literary muscles and the greater your skill will be.

Writing is a journey which promises no clear destination.

Rather, it provides a route to beyond the far horizon that will be as magical as it is unexpected.

Experimenting
Writing is about being creative and experimenting, and is not about laying golden eggs all the time. The problem is that the established publishing model is fixated on making money through selling as many books as possible.

As a result, editors and marketing teams will never green-light anything that's unlikely to pay their salaries.

The one thing publishers detest more than anything else is risk.

As far as they're concerned experimenting is **<u>RISK</u>** – in bold capital letters, underlined. They want travel writers to be writing travel, novelists to be writing novels, and everyone else to be working away in their groove. A publisher's best-case scenario is for their stable of enslaved authors to be writing the same book over and over, so as to extract every ounce of gold from the motherlode.

Writer's Block
Writer's block is a subject I find myself questioning.

I'll explain why.

I was raised in the company of people who wrote professionally. Almost every one of them saw themselves as a basket weaver, a carpenter, or as part of a creative guild. They created to sell their wares in the market, but foremost so as to please themselves.

I once asked Doris for her opinion on writer's block.

She said: 'There's no need to ever get that condition at all. The way to steer clear of it is to think of yourself as a conduit channelling water from the mountains down to the village on the plain. Even though you are the pipe, forget that you are, and concentrate instead on the water flowing through you.'

All Talk
In my opinion, writers should write and not talk.

By that I mean they shouldn't be ranting on at dinner parties or to strangers in the Starbucks queue about how they're working on the next big literary thing. By talking you sap your creative energy and lose the most precious thing of all – literary spontaneity, the magic dust of creativity. Even though you may have planned a book down to the last comma, the joy of writing is going off-piste and delighting yourself with the ride.

First Book
When you haven't written a book before you'll find telling people about it will elicit a frenzy of mostly nonsensical opinions.

Some people will rant on that you're not up to it, or that you'd be better off getting a day job. Others will damn you with faint praise, and sow the seed of doubt. The only way to shut them all up is to finish the book and then write another, and another.

Until you've got to the end of the first book and had it published, it's best to surround yourself with people who share a belief in your skill. I'm not sure why, but general society seems structured towards doubt rather than enthusiasm.

I remember writing the first paragraph of my very first book, thinking to myself:

'It's never again going to be harder than this.'

And it wasn't.

Starting Afresh
As with everything else, starting new projects differs from writer to writer.

The very best time to start writing a new book is the day you finish writing one. Having just typed in the words 'The End', you're probably at the top of your game in terms of enthusiasm and self-confidence. More importantly, the journey through the just-finished book has got you fabulously warmed up.

My advice is to have a new book planned out and ready while you're writing the last third of the current book. There's no question you won't finish the book you're working on, as you've already broken the back of it. Given this, allow yourself a day of change. Use it to work out a new storyline, characters, and nail down a reason to write it – one that'll keep you sucked in over the weeks to come.

Then, in the two or three days before finishing the current project, start making the shift in your head. Obviously, don't make the shift so greatly that you lose the momentum needed to get to the finish line.

Then, on the final day, write the ending of the book at hand.

Congratulate yourself, take a deep breath, and tap out the opening paragraph of the next book...

First footsteps towards the next horizon.

Vocabulary Variety

In writing a book it's easy to run out of fresh words. It sounds crazy, but it happens.

What I mean is that you find you've used all the obvious adjectives and nouns (the low-hanging literary fruit), and to use them again within a stretch of a few pages would be repetition.

There's nothing wrong with repetition, especially if it means keeping things fast-flowing. And I'm not for a moment suggesting using overly obscure words rather than repeating common ones.

My rule of thumb is that if I've used a word twice on the same page, it's easiest to swap it for something else at the first usage. If a thesaurus can't get you a suitable alternative, you may have to resort to changing the sentence construction.

If you've used the same word three times on a page then try changing the second usage.

Ticking Over

The hardest thing to do in the book-writing business is to get back into the saddle when you haven't been writing for a while. Always remember that however long you've left it you can get back to where you were.

No question of that.

Have faith in yourself and you should be able to slip back within a few pages. The key thing is not to read those initial 'brown water' pages back and judge yourself on them.

Instead, keep writing.

If at all possible, don't allow yourself to cool down, because warming up takes time and causes anxiety.

A great way to stay primed up is to write regular letters or emails packed with anecdotes to family and friends. What I tend to do (I'm rather embarrassed to admit this) is to write the same anecdote to a dozen people. Each time I write it, I polish it a little more, or turn it into the light in a new way. By doing this I create a kind of sampler, an experimentation.

And, most importantly of all, I get that warm glow of satisfaction, even if it's in a micro way.

The Tingle

The tingle down the spine you get while reading back what you've written is what writers dream of – or at least I do.

When I started out, it was hit and miss, or rather *miss, miss, miss*.

Then, little by little I learned what ingredients to throw together into the stew in order to get the effect I was after.

There's no sure-fire way to elicit the tingle. I find myself comparing the tingle with making wine. Although vintners rely on good soil, water, grapes, and decades of experience, the final product comes down to something bordering more on alchemy than on science.

The other point to note is there are different kinds of tingle.

A good one is when you've just written something and read it back for the first time.

A better one is when you get it on reading the passage typeset.

The best tingle of all is experienced when reading a book you wrote decades ago.

Thinking Big
Something rooted deep inside me has always urged me to think big, or rather bigger than big.

I just can't help myself.

It would be so much easier for me to drift through life beavering away at small projects, but the universe has conspired for me to reach far and high. As a result of this delusional calibration, I have dozens of books in the pipeline at any one time.

It's worth remembering here that I am writing for myself. And, although it will always be published, I have no intention to please readers or publishers – only myself.

The great thing about releasing work directly as I do is that you can design projects from the ground up and grow them in entirety, exactly as you want. In the same way that Andy Warhol had 'The Factory', the writer who releases work directly can experiment on any scale they like, trying their hand at any genre or technique.

By keeping a grip on how you want your body of work to be shaped and released, you have the ability to succeed in doing what few if any writers have been able to do for two hundred years.

Reading Aloud
A lot of these notes could easily be passed by, but this one is especially important.

Just as people read books in different ways, the same page can seem quite different depending on how the same person reads it. You may not realize it, but when you read text in your head you're doing so in a third-rate way.

Try reading your work aloud.

It alters the dynamic completely, providing a sense of tempo which silent reading can never even come close to achieving. It will highlight the bumps in the road, pointing out faulty construction and grammar.

Best of all though, reading work in progress aloud (to yourself rather than to an audience) will remind you that you have what it takes to be the real writer you're dreaming of being.

Dedications

My father rarely if ever dedicated his work, but my grandfather liked nothing more than doing so. The majority of his books are dedicated to those who helped or inspired him.

When it comes to dedications, I go through phases.

Over the years I've dedicated books to members of my family, close friends, and to a handful of others. When I dedicate a work, I don't simply think of a name to type in at the front.

I write that book for the person.

Putting a photograph of them on my desk, I keep it there and turn to it endlessly as I go. As I proceed, I think about that person as much as I do the book's storyline.

Whispering

This is something I've never actually spoken about, and so have no idea whether it's normal or if I'm stark raving mad. As I progress, formulating sentences in my head, ferrying them down to my fingers to type, I whisper them under my breath as I go. If they sound right in the whisper, then they're likely to read right on the page.

Book Launches

Twenty years ago, all my writer friends and I did launches.

They were opportunities for self-praise and celebration. I've noticed that, as the fortunes of publishers have nosedived, and as the power of the internet has soared, fewer and fewer real writers do launches any longer. This may well be due to the fact authors now have fans all over the world, and that virtual launches make more sense.

I haven't done a book launch in almost a decade. The reason isn't that I've become jaded with publishers, but because I prefer to spend my time writing books rather than having to make small talk over mouthwash wine.

Signings

Unlike book launches – which I'm generally down on – book signings fulfil a function.

The bookshop will order in copies of your work, and do their best to lure their regular clientele to an event. They usually ask a writer to say a few words, after which your latest offering is piled high for the attendees to buy and for you to sign.

The great thing about books made for sale at events is that they can't be returned to the publisher once they've been signed. While you're at a bookshop for a signing, make sure you sign any copies of your book which went unsold.

Festivals

Although in recent years book launches have waned, literary festivals have gone from strength to strength. The most popular festivals, like the one at Cheltenham, have been franchised, with their subsidiaries spanning the world.

I'm always surprised how even the bestselling authors out there get coerced into doing the festival circuit. I suppose many of them don't have a choice. After all, most are owned lock, stock, and barrel by their publishers.

All that, of course, is changing fast.

Pipeline

I've described how I tend to keep the pipeline of projects well filled.

A packed pipeline is incredibly important to me because it means I stay productive. I'm manic when it comes to feeding the pipeline with book ideas. At any one time I'll have dozens of ideas ready to go. Some of them may never see the light of day, while others will start as one thing and eventually become something else.

The pipeline is something I tend to keep to myself because I don't want to hear anyone's opinion on what direction I ought to take.

Beating Oneself Up

In other books I've written about how my life is constructed on a bedrock of guilt.

I feel guilt-ridden at raiding the fridge in the middle of the night, at watching daytime TV, at buying as many useless gadgets as I do on Amazon, and at not producing as much work as I should.

This last reason for guilt hangs heavy over me much of the time.

There's a devil on my shoulder cracking a whip, lambasting me for what he insists is such a derisory output. Some days – especially when it's grey outside – I feel shell-shocked and broken. I know it's absurd, but it happens again and again.

Please learn from the way I tear into myself needlessly and see it doesn't serve any productive use at all. If you can manage to be a ship sailing towards a distant horizon over a glassy sea, then you'll succeed no matter what.

Letters

From time to time, I've written a series of letters between characters (such as in my novel *Timbuctoo*). I've resorted to letters especially when I wasn't quite sure how to add depth to characters. I adore writing letters, and so setting myself the task of conjuring them in a voice other than my own gives me enormous satisfaction.

Conventional publishers tend to strike a long red diagonal editorial line through letters because they tend to believe the technique breaks up a narrative.

On the contrary, my thinking is that letters complement a text, especially if a correspondence is peppered through an entire book.

Gut-think

Like many authors, I get hundreds of emails a week from people asking for advice.

Most of the time my overriding suggestion is not what new writers want to hear. But I dispense it all the same…

Follow your gut.

Think about it for a moment.

You know what you like, what you want to say, and where you want to go. You can lay it all down for me to see, but I'm still never going to get the same three-dimensional grasp of the situation you have right now. Certainly talk to people, ask them for their thoughts, but only do so once you've really examined how you feel yourself.

Stop being frightened about what an agent or publisher will think.

To hell with them!

What matters is YOU.

The book you're going to write will be in your voice, and your voice alone, so it should be a book written by following your gut.

Clatter

My childhood was played out to the sound of a typewriter clattering down in my father's study. As I've often said, the noise never stopped, not for a minute. That's the reason my father left millions of words of print, and at least as much again to be released in the decades after his death.

When I once asked him what the tools of a writer were, he held up his index fingers.

'These are my tools,' he said. 'If they stop working, and that machine over there stops clattering, then the books stop getting written.'

I often think of the comment.

And, when I am working, I listen to the sound of my fingers typing. Tapping away on a keyboard may be less noisy than on a typewriter, but it's essentially the same thing. There's nothing quite so delicious as seeing letters slipping onto a screen. Forming into words, they're like droplets of mercury fusing together...

Words conjured from the furthest reaches of an author's imagination.

Gunpoint

One of the most pressing questions I have about human society is why, when it comes to creative people, such low expectations prevail. We're reminded endlessly of the household names – the Shakespeares, Hugos, Tolstoys, and Goethes – but we're never expected to rival them in the quality or quantity of our own output. It's as if they're in a separate pantheon of their own, and God help anyone who thinks they have even an outside chance at creating anything half as good.

The literary world's dumbing down of anyone trying to break into the world of writing leads to chronically low self-esteem. I've met a great many aspiring authors who don't push themselves because they're just too fearful – of agents, publishers, critics, and readers, too.

Twenty years ago I inherited a box of papers left by my grandfather, The Sirdar Ikbal Ali Shah. Inside I found a treasure trove of material – most of it notes from his travels through Arabia in the 1930s. On a little scrap of paper I found a single line typed out, and saved it – as though it was exceedingly important.

It said:

WRITE AS THOUGH A GUN IS POINTING TO YOUR HEAD

As chance would have it, my Swedish film crew and I were arrested in Pakistan shortly afterwards. Blindfolded and manacled, we were taken to a torture prison, where we spent sixteen dreadful days and nights. Early during the ordeal I was dragged outside in the middle of the night.

A pistol was pressed against the side of my head, and I was told the end of my life had come. As it turned out, the execution was a mock one, laid on to destabilize me... which it did.

The reason I mention it here is that, although intensely unpleasant, having a gun at my head did wonders to focus my thoughts.

Last week a writer friend asked me why I feel it necessary to churn out so much work. I replied it was because I pretend there's a gun to my head and that if I don't grind away – as many other writers should or at least could be doing – the trigger will be pulled.

'Yeah, but it's OK for you, isn't it?' my friend snapped.

'In what way?'

'Well, you've got a first-rate sense of imagination, so you can just close your eyes and see it.'

'See what?'

'See the gun at your head.'

'This is one case in which no imagination is necessary,' I replied.

Steenbeck

My friend, the film-maker Leon Flamholc, was trained to edit movies on a flatbed editing machine known as a Steenbeck.

A complex series of spools routed the film in such a way that the editor could splice exactly where wanted. Leon used to describe the process of editing on a Steenbeck. He would say it was so complex he never imagined ever being able to master the machine.

But with time he became an expert.

'I used to look down at my hands working so fast that they were blurred,' he once explained. 'It was as if I was completely detached, as though they weren't my hands at all.'

When I asked Leon for the secret of mastering the Steenbeck, he said:

'The only way to conquer it was to do it without thinking. If I thought too hard then I'd lose concentration and film would fly out everywhere!'

The same goes for writing books.

Do it in the right way and the book gets written. Think about it too much and you'll get sucked down into the vortex, and your precious work will end up on the mountain of books that were never written.

Parking a Project

One of the things I've been good at in my writing career is finishing the books I start.

There's no doubt it's easier to hammer out a book when it's been commissioned, and all the more pleasing when you've been paid a big, fat advance.

From time to time I've stopped working on a book and parked it. There's no shame at all in stopping work on a book, even when it's well advanced.

The key thing is to place it into a holding pattern, so that you return to it when you're ready. If you find yourself having to halt, make a clear mental note of why you are stopping and how you got into the predicament you're in.

Before moving on to something else, make a vow to yourself to go back to the parked project when you're ready.

Commitment

One of my friends is an exceptional linguist. He speaks at least ten languages fluently, and sucks up foreign grammar and vocabulary like a sponge. One evening at a dinner I drew attention to his remarkable ability to master new languages. Rather than taking the compliment quietly he barked something that's stayed with me:

'The reason I learn languages as I do,' he said, 'is because I put in twelve hours a day hard grind. People always assume I'm some kind of linguistic miracle-worker, but I'm not. The difference between me and all the others who fail at a new language is commitment, and nothing else!'

The same couldn't be more true for book writing.

Almost everyone I meet tells me they dream of having their name on the cover of a book. The answer is they could easily do it, especially given the new publishing technology, but that most of them will fail because they aren't ready to apply themselves.

Dialogue

Some authors smother their dialogue with scaffolding and supports. I am drawn to conversation which is clear, sharp, and has the strength to stand on its own. My suggestion is to lay it as bare as possible, and to trim away anything preventing the words from being heard.

I remember reading Bruce Chatwin's dialogue for the first time and thinking to myself, 'Hoorah! I can hear the characters rather than the writer!' Chatwin achieved this (and I have copied him in almost all my books) by stripping a conversation down to the bare metal.

What works for me is to use a standard set-up for dialogue that's hopefully so subtle the reader hardly even notices it. The structure is no more than a picture frame holding the picture, and is in itself unimportant.

Learning the Ropes

The main reason authors stress about their work is inexperience. In the same way, the very best method of gaining the experience needed to craft different kinds of work is to experiment.

As I said earlier, I was at one time stressed beyond belief at the thought of writing a fight scene. So what I did was to study the best fight scene I could find. It's from the screenplay of *The Princess Bride*, in which Westley duels with Inigo Montoya.

Studying it, and observing it in an almost clinical way, I worked out why the scene was such a triumph on all levels. I've done the same for every challenge that hits my desk – whether it be for description, dialogue, or plot structure, or any other element of the writing process.

Priming

I find the first thousand words of the day are the hardest to get down. It's as though the water pipe has got blocked up in the night, and that every little thing adds to the logjam.

I've isolated two clear ways to get around this, enabling forward movement.

The first is to prime myself by writing something purely pleasurable – like an email or a long, descriptive letter to an old friend. I only start this having read the last page of work, so that my mind is grinding away in the background, thinking about the book on hand. Or if I'm working on a novel, I might write a letter from one character to another, even if I don't have any plan to ever use it in the manuscript. After five or six hundred words I'm in my stride, and am ready to get back to the coal face.

The other priming mechanism I use all the time is to finish a day in the writing chair by setting things up well for the next morning. This entails not only getting the desk tidied up, but leaving the coal face prepped. Even though I'll be in my flow at the end of a day, ready to write almost anything with relative ease, I'll stop short.

As though poised at the top of a steep hill, I'll leave it, to ski down first thing in the morning.

Loving Writing

This may sound crazy, but there's only one reason to write:

BECAUSE YOU LOVE IT

If you don't love it – and I mean REALLY love it – then there's no reason to do it. Agreed, a lot of the time an author's lot is a rough one, fraught with uncertainty and doubt. But it's one of the most extraordinarily creative mediums humanity has yet devised.

In the years I've been writing I have at times found myself forced to do work which bores me senseless. This has included many hundreds of magazine pieces, and a guidebook that reduced me to a whimpering lump of despair.

Even though I was kicking and screaming at the time, each challenge taught me something of great value – forcing me to think in new ways. The more material I've written and published, the more I've found myself on a wide, sprawling plateau…

The Plateau of Sublime Fulfilment.

Standing in the middle of it I feel happy in a deep-down way, as if writing is a best friend, one who's always with me. Get to that point, think of writing as a saviour rather than a demon to be tamed, and your work changes in a profound and inexplicable way.

Literary Seeds

As real writers we are on the lookout for fragments of inspiration, curiosity, and wonder that can be woven into the pages we write.

When it comes to unearthing intriguing details and information, I've always had a pretty good sense. Whether I like it or not my ears and my eyes are always homed in.

For instance, last night I was reading the news online when a curious photo caught my eye: a well-known river in the south-west of England had turned fluorescent blue. Droves of scientists were doing their best to work out the cause of the change in colour.

At seeing the picture many people might have raised an eyebrow before moving on. But the image rooted itself in my mind – just as the one of prosthetic eyes had done. So I noted it down, and worked out how to use it… naturally as a mysterious machination of a rogue jinn.

Contracts

First-time authors are invariably so excited to get a publishing deal, they're ready to sign anything if it means their manuscript is magically transformed into a published book.

Any established writer is likely to dish out the same advice as I'm about to do:

Get a professional to look through the contract and make sure you're protected.

If you have an agent, it's their job to fight your corner.

If you don't have an agent, it's worth joining an association like the Society of Authors, which reviews contracts. The good thing about them is that they tend to be impartial, and are in a position to give advice on how your contract reads compared with others they've seen from the same publisher.

As you can imagine, contracts are all about the terms, and getting the most favourable terms possible.

Advances and royalties are the main meat of the contract business, but there are plenty of smaller clauses you can get amended relatively easily. For example, mainstream publishers tend to offer an author a derisory number of printed books – often as few as six. I've always insisted on getting at least forty copies of every edition. Publishers almost always cave in on author copies as it's something which costs them next to nothing.

Contracts can be a minefield as all kinds of sneaky clauses can be buried deep.

The first key point to beware of is the reversion of rights. This means if your book goes out of print, the rights come back to you. Until recently this wasn't an issue, because publishers had to choose to reprint a stock of the title, or not. But now, with print-on-demand (POD), what publishers do is to put their backlists on the POD system – so that technically they'll never go out of print. As a result, well-meaning authors are locked into the contract forever.

Another tricky clause to watch out for relates to territories. If you're a first-time author, especially one without an agent, the publisher is going to want to suck up all the rights in all territories.

If you have an agent, they will probably want to break the rights of your work down and sell them off bit by bit, like slices of pizza. The more foreign and subsidiary rights they dispose of, the more cold hard cash they make.

When signing a contract, my advice is to only part with British, American, or whatever rights apply to the territory in which you live. Try to keep hold of the other rights, and don't be afraid to cross out wording you don't like. Later on, if the book does well, you could stand to make many times your initial advance through selling foreign rights.

Foreign Rights

I was going to say a good literary agent is the person to sell foreign rights. But times are changing, and they're changing fast!

There are plenty of agents who are lousy at selling foreign rights – largely because they are concentrating on fewer books, but bigger ones. If your book falls into a particular genre – such as chick-lit, fantasy, or detective fiction – you'd do well to spend some time online checking the market out.

All over the world there's an abundance of literary festivals and book fairs at which key publishers in specific genres are represented. Even if you don't have time and money to get to one of these gatherings, you will find the names of the participating publishers, agents, and authors, online.

Foreign language publishers can be found at most book fairs and are generally quite happy to deal directly with English-language authors. They're always on the lookout for published books whose foreign rights are available.

Film Rights and Options

Foreign rights can be a nice little earner, just as selling the film option can be a gravy train which runs on and on.

An option is essentially a fee paid to lock down your book for a given length of time, while a producer tries to raise the finances to make it into a movie. I know dozens of writers, almost all of whom have sold options time and again. Having said that, in very few cases has the movie actually been produced.

Reviews

There was a time when book reviews were everything, and book reviewers were treated like royalty.

In the old days a book would get a tiny window of attention – in which it had to be hyped, reviewed, and piled high in shops.

As with so much, Amazon rewrote the rule book.

There's no longer the manic need to get media attention for a newly launched book in a single week as there used to be. Reviews are still important for writers (especially if they're favourable), but not necessarily newspaper reviews.

More important these days are websites like Goodreads, and others where real readers congregate and share their thinking on new and existing work.

The only reason to want reviews in leading media sources is to extract choice publicity quotes to put on the back of a new edition.

As already noted, print-on-demand platforms make it very easy to update book covers at the drop of the hat with a splash of good publicity.

A last point worth making concerns book reviews themselves.

Although I personally steer clear of reading reviews – whether they're good or bad – even unfavourable reviews sell books.

Dictating

When working on my novel *Hannibal Fogg and the Supreme Secret of Man*, I was writing such long hours I got to a point at which I couldn't get out of the chair.

For my back, and my sanity, I downloaded a dictation program, so I could speak the book onto the screen. Curiously, I found the dictation software could only keep up when the sentences were complicated. When dictating simple sentences, the program got hopelessly confused. Even though my typing is terrible, I eventually got so frustrated with the dictation program that I ditched it and went back to two-finger typing.

Agents

In the days of sky-high book advances literary agents had a key role to play, and they played it well.

As much showmen as they were anything else, they could conjure the smell of the bacon… or, rather, the scent of a bestseller-to-be.

A handful of years ago, publishing had reached a point at which publishers were getting so many submissions that most insisted that authors go through an agent. That was the moment at which agents became gatekeepers, their self-importance mushrooming overnight.

The key point about agents is that they are working for you.

As such, you mustn't be frightened to hire and fire – even though they act as though they're doing you a favour... which they're not.

Unless you've just written the biggest blockbuster fantasy novel in history, an agent will never go into battle for you against a publisher. This is because, while they're trying to sell your masterwork to the editorial and marketing teams, they're also trying to offload dozens of other authors on their books.

The only certainty regarding agents is that in publishing's brave new world there'll be no place for them at all.

Blithering Idiots
Commissioning editors are supposed to edit.

That may sound pretty obvious, but it's not.

Although editors did tend to edit until a few years ago, and were often mini potentates in their own right, they're largely sidelined now from their original role. These days most editors do very little hands-on editing – which is more often than not farmed out to freelancers. The result is that, physically speaking, books have turned from being content-based, to container-based. Shaped by marketing teams, they've become blaring bling-bling objects that scream out at you like packets of breakfast cereal, rather than works of literary merit.

Now, in its last days, the marketing departments hold the real power in the existing model. They have the final word on whether to buy a manuscript, the author's advance, how and when the book will be launched, priced, and what it'll look like.

What I'm about to say next isn't going to win me any friends in the publishing world, but I've long since passed the point at which I cared.

So here it is, loud and clear:

For decades, mainstream publishing has given jobs to people my father used to call 'blithering idiots'. Tens of thousands of them over numerous generations. Nice people, but blithering and idiotic all the same – just like those who were once dispatched to the farthest corners of the empire because they were so incapable.

The existing model – the one that's creaking, straining, and collapsing – sees publishers release tens of thousands of books a year. Almost everything published is destined to fail, with millions of tonnes of newly printed books pulped every year. There's no other line of business I can think of with such a poor return on products.

Publishers may rant that only they have the track record to select books which will be winners. Absolute nonsense of course. In their desperation to make mountains of cash they commission work which is as wretched to read as it is badly printed.

In the brave new world where self-released books are the norm, readers will find themselves feasting on the most extraordinary stories available – stories that don't tick any of the boxes existing publishers hold dear...

Stories which are fresh, original, and unlike anything anyone has read before.

Literary Prizes
Near the end of her life, our family friend, the novelist Doris Lessing, won a Nobel Prize for Literature. Although bemused, she wasn't overly impressed – with the award, the insatiable media attention, or the way the honour recalibrated perceptions of her.

Although I was living in Morocco at the time Doris won the Nobel, I used to drop by and see her whenever I visited England. Her home at 24 Gondar Gardens in London's West Hampstead overflowed with cats, books, and mess.

One afternoon, while sitting at the kitchen table, Doris moaned about the 'damned medal' as though it had brought nothing but trouble. She explained that the prize prevented her from writing, and had allowed the worst kind of people to beat a path to her door.

'The Nobel Prize isn't about me,' she said in an uncharacteristically forlorn voice, 'it's Nobel and nothing else.'

In the years since Doris departed, I've thought about that comment frequently.

She was so incredibly right.

Secret of Writing

When my father had been writing books for thirty years, he said he had something to pass on to me.

I asked what it was.

'The Secret of Writing,' he said.

'What is it?'

'Anecdotes.'

'*Anecdotes*? Is that it?'

'Yes.'

'Why?'

'Because anecdotes are stories and, however hard they try, humans can't resist them. Fill your books with anecdotes and two things will happen. The first is that the books will write themselves. The second is that your readers will devour your work as though it's a delicious sweetmeat.'

Now I'm the one who's been writing books for thirty years, and it's I who've just passed the advice on to my own children – Ariane and Timur.

Cologne

In this book I've included a lot of tricks of the trade I live by. They're very much *my* tricks of the trade though, which I've developed over many years.

This entry is especially close to my heart and is one I swear by. Having said that, it's something I've never told anyone before.

When sitting down to write a new book, I place a bottle of cologne to the right of my computer screen. In most cases it's not my preferred cologne. Indeed, quite often it's a scent I dislike, perhaps a bottle someone gave me for Christmas which got tidied away into a cupboard under the sink.

Before I start working each morning, I dab a few drops of the cologne on the inside of my wrists, breathe the aroma into my lungs, close my eyes, relax, and then begin...

Two or three times through the day I'll open the bottle, dab a few drops, smell it with closed eyes, while I recalibrate.

Like many people I am very sensitive to smells, and find that rooting a project to a particular scent enables me to slip back easily into the writing zone.

I know of writers who play a favourite piece of music before they get down to work, or others who eat a handful of nuts or dates. Whatever the ritual, the effect should return one's mind to the point at which creation begins.

Grammar

I don't remember being drilled in grammar at school – possibly because I was so zoned out. But I'm pretty sure no one ever bothered to teach it in English class, although they did in the endless Latin lessons.

His monocle in place, Major Smith used to bark a sentence in Latin, and we'd have to provide the English translation for fear of being beaten. The result was that I learned English grammar as a kind of by-product of dissecting the Latin text's grammar, as part of the process of translating into English.

Writing prose is a chance to break the rules they tried to grind into me at school. Knowing the rules allows me to break them all the more effectively. Where possible, I do my best to keep sentence structure straightforward. Of course I vary it so as not to put my readers to sleep. But I find that writers who perform endless grammatical pirouettes risk no one accessing their work in a meaningful way.

Chess

A friend who is an especially gifted chess player once commented to me that 'there's always one move that's right, far more so than any other'. The comment has rooted in my mind, not so much for chess – a game in which I do not excel – but for writing.

Authors sit at their desks creating text from letters, words, and paragraphs.

In the course of a day we are faced with thousands of choices...

Choices of a particular word, grammatical structure, punctuation, or literary techniques by which to deliver the story. As I flick through the various possibilities I find myself remembering the chess player's advice – that there's always a right move.

In most cases there is.

To unearth it, you have to twist the construction into the light, observing it from different angles.

No Clones

Early in my journey as a writer I discovered something which sounds so obvious no one would ever mention it:

The fact that no two words have the same meaning.

When trawling through a thesaurus for an alternative way to describe something, I bear it in mind. The joy of the English language is the vast variety of similar words, each one very slightly different from the last.

Value of Words

Although I wasn't taught much grammar at school, I had an English master who was obsessed with précis. He'd get his students to distil great chunks of text down to no more than a handful of lines. At the time it was a task we all loathed, but one which taught me something very useful – the value of words.

The same value was reinforced in my days as a feature writer. If you submitted more than they asked for, editors would go nuts. So I learned the skill of packing as much meat in as possible, while trimming away unnecessary fat.

Reading, Writing

People imagine that reading and writing are two parts of the same skill, and that if you're a real writer you are a real reader as well. In my experience I've found reading and writing are completely separate endeavours. Those who read voraciously are not necessarily the same as those who have the skill to write.

This is a matter I dwell on a great deal, particularly as I'm such a slow reader. Everyone expects me to be ploughing my way through dozens of books a week, whereas I simply can't.

Despite my painfully slow reading ability, I'm a fount of creativity, and can easily knock out a blockbuster novel in three weeks.

The point I'd like to make is to forget what others say or think.

You are how you are.

The task before you is to study yourself, see what works and what doesn't work – and use the tools at your disposal to weave literary cloth.

Publishing Runes

As I've said elsewhere, publishers only spend money on publicizing a book if they have shelled out precious funds by way of an advance. Similarly, they won't dish out an advance of any size until they've consulted with the publishing runes – otherwise known as the Nielsen BookScan figures.

Just as everything else in our data-ridden lives, book sales are measured in the most absurdly accurate way. The data collection company, Nielsen, produce a series of statistics known as 'BookScan', and it's these which are the runes.

In the old days an editor may well have taken a gamble on an unusual book. But publishers ceased their casino ways years ago. Before an editor commissions a book, or buys a finished one in, they'll check the author's previous sales figures. And, if the book is on a specific subject, they'll check how other recent titles in the genre have done.

The danger is of course that if your previous titles sold modestly, the marketing team are unlikely to sanction a big, fat advance.

The one intriguing thing is when a writer has no track record at all. It's rather like *Being There*, the movie in which Peter Sellers stars as Chance the gardener who's lived in isolation his entire life. There's no dirt on him, which means he's the perfect candidate to be president. In the same way, a first-time author is in an extraordinary position.

With no BookScan figures on you, you're a clean sheet.

Tweaking

Although most writers have their own preferred system of writing and editing, the majority rely on some form of tweaking. I tend to get the first draft down so it's there, as if chipped out onto stone. Once it's down no one can ever take it away from me, and it's then I can start tweaking.

What I've found works best is to go through the first draft in a micro way, beavering at each sentence until it's balanced. After that I usually tend to go through it again, and then a third time, before having an editor make corrections.

During the process, the text changes considerably, as individual words are updated, and the structure of the sentences is tweaked.

To give a limited idea of what I mean, I'll write a couple of sentences below, and rework them as I would when editing:

Draft 1
Wilson Marfott was a grim-faced man of fifty, who had no time or interest when it came to dogs. He lived in a lean-to at the edge of the woods, and drank a tumbler of Scotch on the porch each evening as dusk melted into night.

Draft 2
A grim-faced man of fifty, Wilson Marfott had no time or interest for people or for dogs. His home was a shack at the edge of the woods on whose porch he would sit, watch the world, and think. Leaning back on his chair, he'd sip from a tumbler of Scotch as afternoon slipped towards dusk, and dusk into night.

Draft 3
A grim-faced man of fifty, Wilson Marfott had no time or interest for people or for dogs. His home was a shack at the edge of the woods. On its porch he would sit, watch the world, and remember his youth. Leaning back on his chair, he'd stare out sipping whiskey, the afternoon slipping towards dusk, dusk into night.

Finishing Up
We've all known would-be writers who rant on and on how they're working on a book.

Most of the time they're in need of attention and have no real plans to write a book at all. And that's fine by me. But I wish they'd do something that would cut to the chase instead and get them the attention they so badly need.

Once in a long while I've started a book but not finished it. The way I see it, crossing the finish line is part of the book-writing arc. By setting out on the adventure of writing a book you're entering into a solemn covenant with yourself. It's true that with the conventional publishing model the covenant (or rather the contract) is usually with the publisher.

But in my experience there's nothing quite so momentous as making a pact with oneself. As for keeping going, my advice is to make every writing day an adventure, and enjoy every line. If you're not loving the writing process, you're in danger of putting your readers to sleep. And, rather than training your gaze on the finish line, focus on the distant horizon instead. Work towards the far-off destination, and stop thinking about it and how much there is to do.

My overall advice is to know where you want the story to end and to work towards it, even if you're not quite sure of the overall plot. When possible, I like to link the ending back to the beginning, although you can't use that trick every time. I like to have a delicious final line in my head, or at least a scene which caps everything off. Then again, it's also fun to end at another beginning.

The last pages of a book are an exercise in fitting the final pieces into a jigsaw puzzle.

For days and weeks of the writing process it's been plain sailing. You can slot in random ideas, dialogue, procrastinations, and deviations, but suddenly you find yourself on the home straight. That means you have to wake up and move deftly to cover the bases necessary to draw it all together.

As I near the ending of a book I usually come up with a final line – the end equivalent to the foundation stone that started my story. Sometimes I'll print the line out and tape it to my computer monitor, working my way towards it as I go. There's such satisfaction writing the final page of a book, working your way to the last line which fits as perfectly as the final fragment of a puzzle.

Although I tend to write books quite fast, doing my best to keep up momentum, I like to savour the last page or two – writing the text with extra-special care. I never attempt the last strides until my brain is well rested, and I know exactly what I want to say, and how I want to say it.

Any fool can start a book, but it takes real skill to end one.

NOTES

www.ingramcontent.com/pod-product-compliance
Lightning Source LLC
Chambersburg PA
CBHW040317240426
43665CB00031B/2973